Genesis

Back to the Bible Study Guides

Judges: Ordinary People, Extraordinary God

Proverbs: The Pursuit of God's Wisdom

John: Face-to-Face with Jesus

Ephesians: Life in God's Family

James: Living Your Faith

Revelation: The Glorified Christ

GENESIS

A GOD OF PURPOSE,
A PEOPLE OF PROMISE

WOODROW KROLL

CROSSWAY BOOKS
WHEATON, ILLINOIS

Genesis: A God of Purpose, A People of Promise

Copyright © 2007 by Back to the Bible

Published by Crossway Books
            a publishing ministry of Good News Publishers
            1300 Crescent Street
            Wheaton, Illinois 60187

Cover photo: iStock

First printing, 2007

Printed in the United States of America

ISBN 13: 978-1-43350-121-0
ISBN 10: 1-43350-121-X

Unless otherwise indicated, all Scripture quotations are taken from *The Holy Bible: English Standard Version.*® Copyright © 2001 by Crossway Bibles, a publishing ministry of Good News Publishers. Used by permission. All rights reserved.

Produced with the assistance of The Livingstone Corporation (www.LivingstoneCorp.com).

Project Staff: Neil Wilson

CH		18	17	16	15	14	13	12	11	10	09	08
15	14	13	12	11	10	9	8	7	6	5	4	3	2	1

Table of Contents

How to Use This Study

Your study of Genesis will have maximum impact if you prayerfully read each day's Scripture passage. Selected passages of Genesis from the English Standard Version are printed before each lesson's reading, so that everything you need is in one place. While we recommend reading the Scripture passage before you read the devotional, some have found it helpful to use the devotional as preparation for reading the Scripture. If you are unfamiliar with the English Standard Version (on which this series of studies is based), you might consider first reading the devotional, then reading the passage again from a different Bible version. This will give you an excellent basis for considering the rest of the lesson.

After each devotional, there are three sections designed to help you better understand and apply the lesson's Scripture passage.

Consider It—Several questions will help you unpack and reflect on the Scripture passage. These could be used for a small group discussion.

Express It—Suggestions for turning the insights from the lesson into prayer.

Go Deeper—The nature of this study makes it important to see the Book of Genesis in the context of other passages and insights from Scripture. This brief section will allow you to consider some of the implications of the day's passage for the central theme of the study (A God of Purpose, A People of Promise) as well as the way it fits with the rest of Scripture.

Starting Everything

God created a beginning. The Bible tells us without argument, explanation or awkwardness that God started everything.

Read Genesis 1:1–2:25

The Creation of the World

1 In the beginning, God created the heavens and the earth. ²The earth was without form and void, and darkness was over the face of the deep. And the Spirit of God was hovering over the face of the waters.

³And God said, "Let there be light," and there was light. ⁴And God saw that the light was good. And God separated the light from the darkness. ⁵God called the light Day, and the darkness he called Night. And there was evening and there was morning, the first day.

⁶And God said, "Let there be an expanse in the midst of the waters, and let it separate the waters from the waters." ⁷And God made the expanse and separated the waters that were under the expanse from the waters that were above the expanse. And it was so. ⁸And God called the expanse Heaven. And there was evening and there was morning, the second day.

⁹And God said, "Let the waters under the heavens be gathered together into one place, and let the dry land appear." And it was so. ¹⁰God called the dry land Earth, and the waters that were gathered together he called Seas. And God saw that it was good.

¹¹And God said, "Let the earth sprout vegetation, plants yielding seed, and fruit trees bearing fruit in which is their seed, each according to its kind, on the earth." And it was so. ¹²The earth brought forth vegetation, plants yielding seed according to their own kinds, and trees bearing fruit in which is their seed, each according to its kind. And God saw that it was good. ¹³And there was evening and there was morning, the third day.

¹⁴And God said, "Let there be lights in the expanse of the heavens to separate

> # Key Verse
>
> *And God saw everything that he had made, and behold, it was very good. And there was evening and there was morning, the sixth day* (Gen. 1:31).

the day from the night. And let them be for signs and for seasons, and for days and years, ¹⁵and let them be lights in the expanse of the heavens to give light upon the earth." And it was so. ¹⁶And God made the two great lights—the greater light to rule the day and the lesser light to rule the night—and the stars. ¹⁷And God set them in the expanse of the heavens to give light on the earth, ¹⁸to rule over the day and over the night, and to separate the light from the darkness. And God saw that it was good. ¹⁹And there was evening and there was morning, the fourth day.

And God said, "Let the waters swarm with swarms of living creatures, and let birds fly above the earth across the expanse of the heavens." ²¹So God created the great sea creatures and every living creature that moves, with which the waters swarm, according to their kinds, and every winged bird according to its kind. And God saw that it was good. ²²And God blessed them, saying, "Be fruitful and multiply and fill the waters in the seas, and let birds multiply on the earth." ²³And there was evening and there was morning, the fifth day.

²⁴And God said, "Let the earth bring forth living creatures according to their kinds—livestock and creeping things and beasts of the earth according to their

kinds." And it was so. ²⁵And God made the beasts of the earth according to their kinds and the livestock according to their kinds, and everything that creeps on the ground according to its kind. And God saw that it was good.

²⁶Then God said, "Let us make man in our image, after our likeness. And let them have dominion over the fish of the sea and over the birds of the heavens and over the livestock and over all the earth and over every creeping thing that creeps on the earth."

²⁷So God created man in his own image,
in the image of God he created him;
male and female he created them.

²⁸And God blessed them. And God said to them, "Be fruitful and multiply and fill the earth and subdue it and have dominion over the fish of the sea and over the birds of the heavens and over every living thing that moves on the earth." ²⁹And God said, "Behold, I have given you every plant yielding seed that is on the face of all the earth, and every tree with seed in its fruit. You shall have them for food. ³⁰And to every beast of the earth and to every bird of the heavens and to everything that creeps on the earth, everything that has the breath of life, I have given every green plant for food." And it was so. ³¹And God saw everything that he had made, and behold, it was very good. And there was evening and there was morning, the sixth day.

The Seventh Day, God Rests

2 Thus the heavens and the earth were finished, and all the host of them. ²And on the seventh day God finished his work that he had done, and he rested on the seventh day from all his work that he had done. ³So God blessed the seventh day and made it holy, because on it God rested from all his work that he had done in creation.

The Creation of Man and Woman

⁴These are the generations
of the heavens and the earth
when they were created,
in the day that the Lord God made
the earth and the heavens.

⁵When no bush of the field was yet in the land and no small plant of the field had yet sprung up—for the Lord God had not caused it to rain on the land, and there was no man to work the ground, ⁶and a mist was going up from the land and was watering the whole face of the ground—⁷then the Lord God formed the man of dust from the ground and breathed into his nostrils the breath of life, and the man became a living creature. ⁸And the Lord God planted a garden in Eden, in the east, and there he put the man whom he had formed. ⁹And out of the ground the Lord God made to spring up every tree that is pleasant to the sight and good for food. The tree of life was in the midst of the garden, and the tree of the knowledge of good and evil.

¹⁰A river flowed out of Eden to water the garden, and there it divided and became four rivers. ¹¹The name of the first is the Pishon. It is the one that flowed around the whole land of Havilah, where there is gold. ¹²And the gold of that land is good; bdellium and onyx stone are there. ¹³The name of the second river is the Gihon. It is the one that flowed around the whole land of Cush. ¹⁴And the name of the third river is the Tigris, which flows east of Assyria. And the fourth river is the Euphrates.

¹⁵The Lord God took the man and put him in the garden of Eden to work it and keep it. ¹⁶And the Lord God commanded the man, saying, "You may surely eat of every tree of the garden, ¹⁷but of the tree of the knowledge of good and evil you shall not eat, for in the day that you eat of it you shall surely die."

¹⁸Then the LORD God said, "It is not good that the man should be alone; I will make him a helper fit for him." ¹⁹Now out of the ground the LORD God had formed every beast of the field and every bird of the heavens and brought them to the man to see what he would call them. And whatever the man called every living creature, that was its name. ²⁰The man gave names to all livestock and to the birds of the heavens and to every beast of the field. But for Adam there was not found a helper fit for him. ²¹So the LORD God caused a deep sleep to fall upon the man, and while he slept took one of his ribs and closed up its place with flesh. ²²And the rib that the LORD God had taken from the man he made into a woman and brought her to the man. ²³Then the man said,

> "This at last is bone of my bones
> and flesh of my flesh;
> she shall be called Woman,
> because she was taken out of Man."

²⁴Therefore a man shall leave his father and his mother and hold fast to his wife, and they shall become one flesh. ²⁵And the man and his wife were both naked and were not ashamed.

Go Deeper

We can only understand what being made in the image of God means by determining who God is. Our journey toward understanding begins with the creation. Psalm 8 parallels Genesis 1, and both define the image of man as being made a little lower than the heavenly beings. Both these chapters tell us that humans have a relationship with God that elevates them above the natural world. It enables us to have dominion over the natural world.

Note the following selected verses from Psalm 8: "O LORD, our Lord, how majestic is your name in all the earth! . . . When I look at your heavens, the work of your fingers, the moon and the stars, which you have set in place, what is man that you are mindful of him, and the son of man that you care for him?. . . O LORD, our Lord, how majestic is your name in all the earth!" (Ps. 8:1, 3–4, 9).

The teaching of man's dominion over nature is a revolutionary concept. Measure it against ancient religions that declared the gods were natural powers and man's life was embraced by this mysterious depth of nature. But the God of Israel is not a natural power. He transcends the realm of nature. He is, in fact, the Creator of all nature.

That's why the Bible begins with God and in some lesser sense, man. Though we're related to the animals, we stand as a representative or kind of a vice-regent of God's sovereignty, His kingdom here on earth. When you pick up your Bible, recognize that the reason the Bible begins with God is very simple. It's because the Bible is all about God.

W hen we open our Bibles to the first page of Genesis, it's like pushing open a weathered and worn door that takes us into an artist's workshop. At first, we hear only echoes and feel only emptiness. We can't see a thing. We realize this is true not only because there is no light but because there is nothing to see. The Artist-Creator is the only presence. But not for long.

God first created a canvas, a place to fashion a great masterpiece—"the heavens and the earth" (Gen. 1:1). But this was no ordinary artist's canvas, stretched and white on an easel. This canvas was "without form and void, and darkness was over the face of the deep. And the Spirit of God was hovering over the face of the waters" (1:2). The Divine Artist brooded over the vast expanse He was about to fill. He considered before He continued to create.

He would fill His masterpiece with good, God decided; and He set about to accomplish His purpose. On the first day of creation, God spoke light into existence. Apparently, God didn't have to create darkness—that was the condition until light began.

In a way that teases our modern scientific mindset, God filled the universe with light several days before He created the "lights in the expanse of the heavens . . . the two great lights—the greater light to rule the day and the lesser light to rule the night—and the stars" (vv. 14, 16). Not only that, but God created a world full of vegetation that lives by photosynthesis the day before He created the sun that would provide the energy for the process! Was this an oversight on the part of the writer of Genesis or a wonderful glimpse at the Source and Center of everything?

For an answer, we can turn to the very end of God's Word, Revelation 21:23 and read, "And the city has no need of sun or moon to shine on it, for the glory of God gives it light, and its lamp is the Lamb." The instant global greenhouse God created on day three didn't need the sun's light because it flourished under the light of the glory of God. Psalm 19:1 isn't kidding when it says, "The heavens declare the glory of God, and the sky above proclaims his handiwork."

God must love patterns and rhythms because He built them into the structure of the universe. The spinning orbs rotate in precise

> **"** *The Bible begins with a message about God and a message about us. He, as the sole Author and Creator, made man and woman unique from the rest of His creation because He has a very special purpose in mind for us.* **"**

patterns that in turn create night and day, ebb and tide. As we watch the days of creation end and begin ("And there was evening and there was morning" (Gen. 1:5, 8, 13, 19, 23, 31), we hear God declare that the results of His creative acts are "good" (1:4, 10, 12, 18, 21, 25, 31). Follow the sequence of God's pattern, and He appears to be making preparations. God's actions lead to the creation of a place where someone will live. He describes that someone as man—created in God's own image. (See v. 27.) With the creation of human beings, God reaches the crown of His creativity. God's pattern had a purpose, and the purpose turned out to be us.

There are five reasons why you are the crown of God's creation. First, if you trace the order of man's creation, you'll find that you're different. You're last but not least, for God gave you a special role as a steward to exercise dominion (responsible use) "over every living thing that moves on the earth" (v. 28).

The second crown-ship claim is based on the unique method of man's creation. All the way up to the end, God used His voice. God spoke everything into existence except men and women. He created man by shaping him from mud and breathing into him the breath of life (2:7). Then woman was taken from that creation into which God breathed the breath of life (vv. 21–22).

Reason three has to do with God's breath. God breathed Himself into humans (2:7). Anything that He breathes into is designed to speak of God to others. In fact, there's only one other thing that is described as "God-breathed"—God's Word. (See 2 Tim. 3:16.)

A fourth reason we are creation's crown is the pattern of our origin. Only humans were created in God's image (Gen. 1:26–27). The image of God imparts special meaning to us, a special harmony with God. It means we've been given a special design and intelligence—we're part of being created in God's image.

The fifth reason for our uniqueness is also in Genesis 1:26. We were created "after our likeness [the likeness of God]." God is not just repeating Himself. These are two similar but distinct terms: image and likeness. The first has to do with traits and abilities; the second with essential makeup. In other words, as God is a tri-person God, a tripartite being—God the Father, God the Son and God the Holy Spirit—we are also tri-persons composed of body, soul and spirit.

The Bible begins with a message about God and a message about us. He, as the sole Author and Creator, made man and woman unique from the rest of His creation because He has a very special purpose in mind for us. We are capable of communicating with God. We're capable of thinking like He thinks. God wants us to be like Him, and He wants us to think like Him. He wants us to tell the world about Him. And so He crowned all of His creation by creating us.

Express It

Romans 1 tells us that when we lose touch with God as Creator, we forget to be grateful. But if all that we are and have comes from God's hands, the least we can do is express our thanks. Put yourself where you can see some of the wonders of God's creation, and thank Him for everything beautiful that you see.

Consider It

As you read Genesis 1:1–2:25, consider these questions:

1) As you begin this study of Genesis, what are your expectations about what you will learn or review in this book?

_____

_____

_____

2) What part of the creation sequence would you most liked to have seen happen?

_____

_____

_____

3) What do we learn about God in these two chapters?

_____

_____

_____

4) What do we learn about ourselves?

_____

_____

_____

5) How does it affect you to know that "God is light, and in him is no darkness at all" (1 John 1:5)?

_____

_____

_____

6) To what degree do you think that Genesis 2:24 accurately describes the ideals in marriage?

_____

_____

_____

7) Based on these two chapters, what are your impressions of Adam and Eve?

_____

_____

_____

Shattered Masterpiece

Despite wishful thoughts to the contrary, one of the undeniable common traits of all humans is our capacity and tendency to sin. We naturally do what we shouldn't do. How did that infection get started?

Read Genesis 3:1–5:32

Genesis 3:1–24

The Fall

3 Now the serpent was more crafty than any other beast of the field that the LORD God had made.

He said to the woman, "Did God actually say, 'You shall not eat of any tree in the garden'?" ²And the woman said to the serpent, "We may eat of the fruit of the trees in the garden, ³but God said, 'You shall not eat of the fruit of the tree that is in the midst of the garden, neither shall you touch it, lest you die.'" ⁴But the serpent said to the woman, "You will not surely die. ⁵For God knows that when you eat of it your eyes will be opened, and you will be like God, knowing good and evil." ⁶So when the woman saw that the tree was good for food, and that it was a delight to the eyes, and that the tree was to be desired to make one wise, she took of its fruit and ate, and she also gave some to her husband who was with her, and he ate. ⁷Then the eyes of both were opened, and they knew that they were naked. And they sewed fig leaves together and made themselves loincloths.

⁸And they heard the sound of the LORD God walking in the garden in the cool of the day, and the man and his wife hid themselves from the presence of the LORD God among the trees of the garden. ⁹But the LORD God called to the man and said to him, "Where are you?" ¹⁰And he said, "I heard the sound of you in the garden, and I was afraid, because I was naked, and I hid myself." ¹¹He said, "Who told you that you were naked? Have you eaten of the tree of which I commanded you not to eat?" ¹²The man said, "The woman whom you gave to be with me, she gave me fruit of the tree, and I ate." ¹³Then the LORD God said to the woman, "What is this that you have done?" The woman said, "The serpent deceived me, and I ate."

Key Verse

Then the eyes of both were opened, and they knew that they were naked. And they sewed fig leaves together and made themselves loincloths (Gen. 3:7).

¹⁴The LORD God said to the serpent,

"Because you have done this,
    cursed are you above all livestock
    and above all beasts of the field;
on your belly you shall go,
    and dust you shall eat
    all the days of your life.
¹⁵I will put enmity between you and
    the woman,
    and between your offspring and
    her offspring;
he shall bruise your head,
    and you shall bruise his heel."

¹⁶To the woman he said,

"I will surely multiply your pain in
    childbearing;
    in pain you shall bring forth
    children.
Your desire shall be for your
husband,
    and he shall rule over you."

¹⁷And to Adam he said,

"Because you have listened to the
    voice of your wife
    and have eaten of the tree
of which I commanded you,
    'You shall not eat of it,'
cursed is the ground because of
you;
    in pain you shall eat of it all the
    days of your life;
¹⁸thorns and thistles it shall bring
    forth for you;

and you shall eat the plants of the field.
¹⁹By the sweat of your face
you shall eat bread,
till you return to the ground,
for out of it you were taken;
for you are dust,
and to dust you shall return."

²⁰The man called his wife's name Eve, because she was the mother of all living. ²¹And the LORD God made for Adam and for his wife garments of skins and clothed them.

²²Then the LORD God said, "Behold, the man has become like one of us in knowing good and evil. Now, lest he reach out his hand and take also of the tree of life and eat, and live forever—" ²³therefore the LORD God sent him out from the garden of Eden to work the ground from which he was taken. ²⁴He drove out the man, and at the east of the garden of Eden he placed the cherubim and a flaming sword that turned every way to guard the way to the tree of life.

Go Deeper

History may look back on our times as the Age of Blame. When anything goes wrong, the first response, even before taking action to fix the problem, is to assign blame. Adam and Eve show us this is a deeply rooted tendency in human beings. One of our tendencies is to read the account of the Fall of humanity and wonder why Adam and not Eve is held responsible in the rest of Scripture. After all, didn't she sin before Adam? Yet Romans 5:12–17 and 1 Corinthians 15:20–22 place responsibility for the Fall squarely on Adam.

Notice in Genesis 3:8–12 that God confronts Adam with the sin of disobedience. Adam gets the blame ball rolling. The key to this issue is found in order of creation and the fact (Gen. 2:15–17) that God gave the command not to eat the fruit of the tree to Adam before Eve was created. It was Adam's job to help his wife understand the danger. When Eve took the fruit, she was challenging Adam's instructions. When Adam joined her in eating the fruit, he challenged God's direct command. They were together in their sin, but Adam had the greater responsibility as the head of mankind.

Chapter 2 of Genesis ends with a picture of marital bliss: "And the man and his wife were both naked and were not ashamed" (v. 25). Unfortunately, their happily-ever-after life was short-lived. Chapter 3 opens with a tone of impending doom. By the time we reach verse 6, we have seen Eve and Adam take four deliberate steps that lead to the shattering of God's masterpiece—creation.

The four self-destructive steps we find in Genesis 3:6 are not merely the original choices that led to our condition as sinners; they also describe choices we make today that lead to problems in our lives.

Step number one in destroying yourself begins with sight: "So when the woman *saw* that the tree was good for food . . ." (emphasis added). The fruit looked delicious. Once the serpent directed her attention to it, she wondered why she hadn't noticed the fine appearance of the fruit on the forbidden tree. But appearances fooled her, just as they fooled other people we read about in Scripture.

Joshua 7 includes the story of Achan and the tragedy that occurred because he acted on appearances. Here's his confession: "And Achan answered Joshua, 'Truly I have sinned against the LORD God of Israel, and this is what I did: when I saw among the spoil . . . then I coveted them and took them. And see, they are hidden in the earth inside my tent, with the silver underneath'" (vv. 20–21).

One of the best known figures in the Old Testament, King David, was tripped up by this same problem. "It happened, late one afternoon, when David arose from his couch and was walking on the roof of the king's house, that he saw from the roof a woman bathing; and the woman was very beautiful" (2 Sam. 11:2). David was engaged in the equivalent of surfing the Internet one evening. He *saw* a scene that instantly drew his attention. He took the first step toward disaster.

Eve's path to self-destruction began with sight. So did Achan's and David's downward journey. We know that sight in and of itself is not sin. Often you can't help what you see. But you can certainly help what you gaze at. You can question your decision to take a second peek.

If step number one toward disaster involves sight, step number two in destroying yourself is desire. Eve couldn't avoid seeing the tree,

"*The path that destroys us is clear. We are prone to follow it in the same ways Eve and Adam followed it so long ago.*"

but she could avoid desiring the fruit of the tree knowing full well that the tree contained forbidden fruit. After what we *see*, *desire* gets us leaning in the wrong direction.

Step three in destroying yourself involves action. It's taking what you know you shouldn't take. Eve took of the fruit of the tree. Achan took the spoils. David took another man's wife.

Step number four in self-destruction has little to do with you and everything to do with others. Step one (Eve saw); step two (Eve desired); step three (Eve ate); and then step four: "She also gave some to her husband who was with her, and he ate" (Gen. 3:6). The fourth step recruits others. There's no such thing as private sin. We always sin and involve others—even in things we do for ourselves or to ourselves. The actions of both Achan and David as well as Eve involved others in a tragedy.

Sin never limits its consequences to the individual sinner. It spreads like a deadly virus. Sin always harms and destroys others. The world may claim "privacy" for sin, but the Bible tells us that we never sin alone, even if no one else is around. Joshua and Israel had to make a complete sacrifice of Achan and all that he had, including his family, to make certain his sin was covered and would not spread like a deadly, infectious virus. David's family was racked with havoc as a result of his sin. And every one of us is affected by Adam and Eve's choice in Eden.

The path that destroys us is clear. We are prone to follow it in the same ways Eve and Adam followed it so long ago. The secret to keep from destroying yourself is to stop wherever you are on the path, turn around and retrace your steps. We have this promise from God: "If we confess our sins, he is faithful and just to forgive us our sins and to cleanse us from all unrighteousness" (1 John 1:9).

Stop destroying yourself and others with you. Confess your sin. Forsake it. Ask God to forgive you for it. And then, start over. This time walk before God and be blameless. You can do it. The Spirit will help you to be strong.

Express It

As you pray, consider your own part in the human lineage. Talk to God about your understanding that you, too, bear unmistakable family characteristics with Adam. Think about the ways God has intervened in your life (as He did in Cain's), and thank Him for the gift of life through Adam and the gift of eternal life through the second Adam—Jesus Christ. In the light of Genesis 3–5, reflect on the good news of John 3:16!

Consider It

As you read Genesis 3:1–5:32, consider these questions:

1) **What examples from your life parallel Eve's "seeing" mistake?**

2) **What spiritual strategy do you use to handle temptation?**

3) **Why do you think Eve was so easily convinced to eat the fruit?**

4) **What makes Adam and Eve's sin such that it's called "the Fall" of humanity?**

5) **How did the presence of sin show itself in the lives of Cain and Abel?**

6) **What opportunity did God give Cain to resist the sin of killing his brother?**

7) **How does the Bible describe human life between the time of Adam and Noah?**

A Man, an Ark and a Flood

One of the fascinating discoveries by anthropologists studying isolated cultures around the world has been the almost universal existence of flood stories. Apparently, humans everywhere still remember that great disaster. But do we know the lesson it teaches?

Read Genesis 6:1–11:26

Genesis 6:1–7:24

Increasing Corruption on Earth

6 When man began to multiply on the face of the land and daughters were born to them, ²the sons of God saw that the daughters of man were attractive. And they took as their wives any they chose. ³Then the LORD said, "My Spirit shall not abide in man forever, for he is flesh: his days shall be 120 years." ⁴The Nephilim were on the earth in those days, and also afterward, when the sons of God came in to the daughters of man and they bore children to them. These were the mighty men who were of old, the men of renown.

⁵The LORD saw that the wickedness of man was great in the earth, and that every intention of the thoughts of his heart was only evil continually. ⁶And the LORD was sorry that he had made man on the earth, and it grieved him to his heart. ⁷So the LORD said, "I will blot out man whom I have created from the face of the land, man and animals and creeping things and birds of the heavens, for I am sorry that I have made them." ⁸But Noah found favor in the eyes of the LORD.

Noah and the Flood

⁹These are the generations of Noah. Noah was a righteous man, blameless in his generation. Noah walked with God. ¹⁰And Noah had three sons, Shem, Ham, and Japheth.

¹¹Now the earth was corrupt in God's sight, and the earth was filled with violence. ¹²And God saw the earth, and behold, it was corrupt, for all flesh had corrupted their way on the earth. ¹³And God said to Noah, "I have determined to make an end of all flesh, for the earth is filled with violence through them. Behold, I will destroy them with the earth. ¹⁴Make yourself an ark of gopher wood. Make rooms in the ark, and cover it inside and out with pitch. ¹⁵This is how you are to make it: the length of the ark 300 cubits, its breadth 50 cubits, and its height 30 cubits. ¹⁶Make a roof for the ark, and finish it to a cubit above, and set the door of the ark in its side. Make it with lower, second, and third decks. ¹⁷For behold, I will bring a flood of waters upon the earth to destroy all flesh in which is the breath of life under heaven. Everything that is on the earth shall die. ¹⁸But I will establish my covenant with you, and you shall come into the ark, you, your sons, your wife, and your sons' wives with you. ¹⁹And of every living thing of all flesh, you shall bring two of every sort into the ark to keep them alive with you. They shall be male and female. ²⁰Of the birds according to their kinds, and of the animals according to their kinds, of every creeping thing of the ground, according to its kind, two of every sort shall come in to you to keep them alive. ²¹Also take with you every sort of food that is eaten, and store it up. It shall serve as food for you and for them." ²²Noah did this; he did all that God commanded him.

7 Then the LORD said to Noah, "Go into the ark, you and all your household, for I have seen that you are righteous before me in this generation. ²Take with you seven pairs of all clean animals, the male and his mate, and a pair of the animals that are not clean, the male and his mate, ³and seven pairs of the birds of the heavens also, male and female,

> ## Key Verse
> *Noah was a righteous man, blameless in his generation. Noah walked with God* (Gen. 6:9).

to keep their offspring alive on the face of all the earth. ⁴For in seven days I will send rain on the earth forty days and forty nights, and every living thing that I have made I will blot out from the face of the ground." ⁵And Noah did all that the Lᴏʀᴅ had commanded him.

⁶Noah was six hundred years old when the flood of waters came upon the earth. ⁷And Noah and his sons and his wife and his sons' wives with him went into the ark to escape the waters of the flood. ⁸Of clean animals, and of animals that are not clean, and of birds, and of everything that creeps on the ground, ⁹two and two, male and female, went into the ark with Noah, as God had commanded Noah. ¹⁰And after seven days the waters of the flood came upon the earth.

¹¹In the six hundredth year of Noah's life, in the second month, on the seventeenth day of the month, on that day all the fountains of the great deep burst forth, and the windows of the heavens were opened. ¹²And rain fell upon the earth forty days and forty nights. ¹³On the very same day Noah and his sons, Shem and Ham and Japheth, and Noah's wife and the three wives of his sons with them entered the ark, ¹⁴they and every beast, according to its kind, and all the livestock according to their kinds, and every creeping thing that creeps on the earth, according to its kind, and every bird, according to its kind, every winged creature. ¹⁵They went into the ark with Noah, two and two of all flesh in which there was the breath of life. ¹⁶And those that entered, male and female of all flesh, went in as God had commanded him. And the Lᴏʀᴅ shut him in.

¹⁷The flood continued forty days on the earth. The waters increased and bore up the ark, and it rose high above the earth. ¹⁸The waters prevailed and increased greatly on the earth, and the ark floated on the face of the waters. ¹⁹And the waters prevailed so mightily on the earth that all the high mountains under the whole heaven were covered. ²⁰The waters prevailed above the mountains, covering them fifteen cubits deep. ²¹And all flesh died that moved on the earth, birds, livestock, beasts, all swarming creatures that swarm on the earth, and all mankind. ²²Everything on the dry land in whose nostrils was the breath of life died. ²³He blotted out every living thing that was on the face of the ground, man and animals and creeping things and birds of the heavens. They were blotted out from the earth. Only Noah was left, and those who were with him in the ark. ²⁴And the waters prevailed on the earth 150 days.

Go Deeper

In the Genesis account, God is a God of morality and ethics. The world has sinned greatly and totally. It has broken the rules. Punishment has to follow. The purpose for the flood in the Genesis account is for distinctly moral judgment, not divine irrationality. God is good, but judgment is necessary.

In the flood we see how God judges. This is an assessment of God's judgment on unchecked wickedness in the world. "And God said to Noah, 'I have determined to make an end of all flesh, for the earth is filled with violence through them. Behold, I will destroy them with the earth'" (Gen. 6:13). Also, "For behold, I will bring a flood of waters

(continued)

Go Deeper Continued . . .

upon the earth to destroy all flesh in which is the breath of life under heaven. Everything that is on the earth shall die" (6:17).

God is gracious and slow to anger. But God is holy and just. And when sin is present, judgment has to follow. The picture of what happened in the days of Noah is an excellent picture of what's happening in our day.

God is being very patient with us. He sees the way people flaunt their sin in His face, and He is waiting. The day will come when the holy God will bring judgment because judgment must always follow unrepented sin. But as you see the unchecked wickedness of the earth and God's assessment of the people on the earth, you have to be struck with God's faithfulness in saving Noah and in offering salvation to us.

Before the famous ark was built, a man named Noah proved himself unique among his peers. He wasn't sinless; he was "blameless." Someone sinless doesn't sin; someone blameless knows what to do when he sins. If Noah was a righteous man who walked with God, then he knew that God can deal with sins through forgiveness. In Noah's day, everyone else had apparently forgotten this.

Following a description of the rampant sin on earth, the Bible adds a note of hope that ought to grab our attention: "But Noah found favor in the eyes of the Lord" (Gen. 6:8). Thus begins the story of a man, a ship and the flood that wiped out human civilization.

God used these events to teach us early history. But the ark was a lot more than the first seafaring vessel; it was an illustration as well. These things happened, the apostle Paul says, as illustrations and lessons for us to learn spiritual truths as well as historical ones. (See 1 Cor. 10:11.)

In the light of God's management of history, Genesis 6:8 becomes even more significant—"But Noah found favor in the eyes of the Lord." Now the word *favor* here means "grace" or "acceptance." (See also Gen. 39:4; Ex. 33:13; Ruth 2:10.) While the word *grace* or *favor* in the Old Testament may not be charged with all the meaning that it has in the New Testament, given the sacrifice of Christ, it nonetheless was understood to mean *favor* for unexplained reasons. Favor isn't earned; it is unexpectedly given.

Noah was not innately righteous. He was merely a man of faith, and he was declared righteous before God because of his faith as a just man in a world of unjust and unfaithful people. Noah made quite an impression. Noah lived righteously in a world that was living unbelievably unrighteously. And as God took note of him, He will do the same with us.

The details of the ark and its construction are familiar and remarkable. The dimensions are exactly correct for a sailing vessel of that size. But then Noah had a divine designer for his ship. God's intimate involvement answers many of the obvious questions that come to mind as we read the account. One is reminded of Jesus' words, "With man this is impossible, but with God all things are possible" (Matt. 19:26). Even the context of Jesus' statement is interesting, since His disciples had just heard Him describe a situation as impossible as a worldwide flood. (See Matt. 19:23–24.) His disciples asked, "Who then can be saved?"

With the eyes of faith, we can see clearly a deeper meaning to the story of Noah's ark. We can see it as an early clue to a repeating theme throughout Scripture. In the ark we will find more than just a boat. We will see God's method of salvation. When we look at Noah's story through the lens of God's great work in history, certain details jump out as significant and symbolic.

First of all, the ark was God's idea, not Noah's idea. Our hero didn't hear the long-range weather report on the radio one day and decide he needed to create an escape vehicle. Faced with an impossible situation, our best hope is always God's intervention. God worked this amazing example of physical salvation to demonstrate His willingness to create a way for our spiritual salvation.

Second, God told Noah to make multiple rooms, rooms enough to house those who were going to be saved. Jesus said, "In my Father's house are many rooms. If it were not so, would I have told you that I go to prepare a place for you? And if I go and prepare a place for you, I will come again and will take you to myself, that where I am you may be also" (John 14:2–3). The same God who told Noah to prepare a floating mansion has prepared a heavenly place for us. God is the architect; He is the builder; He is the Savior.

Third, notice the pitch that made the boat watertight. Without it, Noah's ark would have been just a pile of lumber. The *pitch* was the key to the whole plan. The word used in Hebrew for pitch is the word *kaphar.* And while the word *kaphar* means "to cover with *pitch* or

"In the ark we will find more than just a boat. We will see God's method of salvation. When we look at Noah's story through the lens of God's great work in history, certain details jump out as significant and symbolic."

coat," its most frequent use in the Bible is as the word for atonement. *Kaphar* means "to cover, to purge, to make an atonement, to make reconciliation." It's a word in the Bible for salvation.

The pitch on Noah's boat parallels what the blood of Jesus Christ did for you. It covered your sins. It purged you from them. It made atonement for your sins. It appeased the wrath of God. Christ Jesus did in His death what you could not do in your life. He paid the penalty for your sins. You can float in a world sinking in sin if Jesus covers you.

Finally, did you take note of the fact that there is only one door into the ark? Jesus is that door (John 14:6). God's plan is in place and the way of salvation has been provided. But only through Christ do we gain access to that salvation. We live in a world flooded by sin. Have you accepted God's way of salvation?

Express It

Seeing how God took note of Noah's righteousness and blamelessness can humble us before Him. God's favor (grace) continually moves us toward righteousness and blamelessness. We ought to regularly express our desire for God's grace to do its work in us. That's not a request we should make lightly before the Lord.

Consider It

As you read Genesis 6:1–11:26, consider these questions:

1) How do you think Noah's neighbors felt about the large ship taking shape in Noah's yard far from water?

_____

_____

_____

2) What kind of opportunity did God provide for the people by having Noah construct such a visual warning of judgment?

_____

_____

_____

3) Although none of us lives far from death, how do we tend to respond to warnings and reminders of judgment and life's brevity?

_____

_____

_____

4) What kind of covenant did God establish with Noah and his sons after the flood?

_____

_____

_____

5) In what ways has God faithfully kept that covenant?

_____

_____

_____

6) How do we know that sinfulness survived the flood with Noah's family?

_____

_____

_____

7) What parallels do you see between your life and Noah's story?

_____

_____

_____

The Original Patriarch

The front page of today's newspaper probably includes the Middle East in one or more headlines. How often do we pause to think that a man we know as Abraham was born somewhere in that area many years ago? World history seems divinely rooted in the eastern end of the Mediterranean Sea.

Read Genesis 12:1–14:24

Genesis 12, 14

The Call of Abram

12 Now the LORD said to Abram, "Go from your country and your kindred and your father's house to the land that I will show you. ²And I will make of you a great nation, and I will bless you and make your name great, so that you will be a blessing. ³I will bless those who bless you, and him who dishonors you I will curse, and in you all the families of the earth shall be blessed."

⁴So Abram went, as the LORD had told him, and Lot went with him. Abram was seventy-five years old when he departed from Haran. ⁵And Abram took Sarai his wife, and Lot his brother's son, and all their possessions that they had gathered, and the people that they had acquired in Haran, and they set out to go to the land of Canaan. When they came to the land of Canaan, ⁶Abram passed through the land to the place at Shechem, to the oak of Moreh. At that time the Canaanites were in the land. ⁷Then the LORD appeared to Abram and said, "To your offspring I will give this land." So he built there an altar to the LORD, who had appeared to him. ⁸From there he moved to the hill country on the east of Bethel and pitched his tent, with Bethel on the west and Ai on the east. And there he built an altar to the LORD and called upon the name of the LORD. ⁹And Abram journeyed on, still going toward the Negeb.

Abram and Sarai in Egypt

¹⁰Now there was a famine in the land. So Abram went down to Egypt to sojourn there, for the famine was severe in the land. ¹¹When he was about to enter Egypt, he said to Sarai his wife, "I know that you are a woman beautiful in appearance, ¹²and when the Egyptians see you, they will say, 'This is his wife.'Then they will kill me, but they will

live. ¹³Say you are my sister, that it may go well with me because of you, and that my life may be spared for your sake." ¹⁴When Abram entered Egypt, the Egyptians saw that the woman was very beautiful. ¹⁵And when the princes of Pharaoh saw her, they praised her to Pharaoh. And the woman was taken into Pharaoh's house. ¹⁶And for her sake he dealt well with Abram; and he had sheep, oxen, male donkeys, male servants, female servants, female donkeys, and camels.

¹⁷But the LORD afflicted Pharaoh and his house with great plagues because of Sarai, Abram's wife. ¹⁸So Pharaoh called Abram and said, "What is this you have done to me? Why did you not tell me that she was your wife? ¹⁹Why did you say, 'She is my sister,'so that I took her for my wife? Now then, here is your wife; take her, and go." ²⁰And Pharaoh gave men orders concerning him, and they sent him away with his wife and all that he had.

* * * * * * * * * * * * * *

Abram Rescues Lot

14 In the days of Amraphel king of Shinar, Arioch king of Ellasar, Chedorlaomer king of Elam, and Tidal king of Goiim, ²these kings made war with Bera king of Sodom, Birsha king

> # *Key Verse*
>
> *"And I will make of you a great nation, and I will bless you and make your name great, so that you will be a blessing"* (Gen. 12:2).

of Gomorrah, Shinab king of Admah, Shemeber king of Zeboiim, and the king of Bela (that is, Zoar). ³And all these joined forces in the Valley of Siddim (that is, the Salt Sea). ⁴Twelve years they had served Chedorlaomer, but in the thirteenth year they rebelled. ⁵In the fourteenth year Chedorlaomer and the kings who were with him came and defeated the Rephaim in Ashteroth-karnaim, the Zuzim in Ham, the Emim in Shaveh-kiriathaim, ⁶and the Horites in their hill country of Seir as far as El-paran on the border of the wilderness. ⁷Then they turned back and came to Enmishpat (that is, Kadesh) and defeated all the country of the Amalekites, and also the Amorites who were dwelling in Hazazon-tamar.

⁸Then the king of Sodom, the king of Gomorrah, the king of Admah, the king of Zeboiim, and the king of Bela (that is, Zoar) went out, and they joined battle in the Valley of Siddim ⁹with Chedorlaomer king of Elam, Tidal king of Goiim, Amraphel king of Shinar, and Arioch king of Ellasar, four kings against five. ¹⁰Now the Valley of Siddim was full of bitumen pits, and as the kings of Sodom and Gomorrah fled, some fell into them, and the rest fled to the hill country. ¹¹So the enemy took all the possessions of Sodom and Gomorrah, and all their provisions, and went their way. ¹²They also took Lot, the son of Abram's brother, who was dwelling in Sodom, and his possessions, and went their way.

¹³Then one who had escaped came and told Abram the Hebrew, who was living by the oaks of Mamre the Amorite, brother of Eshcol and of Aner. These were allies of Abram. ¹⁴When Abram heard that his kinsman had been taken captive, he led forth his trained men, born in his house, 318 of them, and went in pursuit as far as Dan. ¹⁵And he divided his forces against them by night, he and his servants, and defeated them and pursued them to Hobah, north of Damascus. ¹⁶Then he brought back all the possessions, and also brought back his kinsman Lot with his possessions, and the women and the people.

Abram Blessed by Melchizedek

¹⁷After his return from the defeat of Chedorlaomer and the kings who were with him, the king of Sodom went out to meet him at the Valley of Shaveh (that is, the King's Valley). ¹⁸And Melchizedek king of Salem brought out bread and wine. (He was priest of God Most High.) ¹⁹And he blessed him and said,

"Blessed be Abram by God Most High,
  Possessor of heaven and earth;
²⁰and blessed be God Most High,
  who has delivered your enemies into your hand!"

And Abram gave him a tenth of everything. ²¹And the king of Sodom said to Abram, "Give me the persons, but take the goods for yourself." ²²But Abram said to the king of Sodom, "I have lifted my hand to the Lord, God Most High, Possessor of heaven and earth, ²³that I would not take a thread or a sandal strap or anything that is yours, lest you should say, 'I have made Abram rich.' ²⁴I will take nothing but what the young men have eaten, and the share of the men who went with me. Let Aner, Eshcol, and Mamre take their share."

Go Deeper

King Melchizedek is mentioned only twice in the Old Testament (Gen. 14:18–20 and Ps. 110:4). In the New Testament, the writer of Hebrews mentions him by name eight times (Heb. 5:6, 10; 6:20; 7:1, 10–11, 15, 17). Reading the passages from Genesis, Psalms and Hebrews at one sitting presents quite a startling picture of the way God works in the world. Not only does Melchizedek serve as a foreshadowing of Christ, he also is living evidence that God had His hand on people outside the Abrahamic family tree.

As you read these passages, consider in particular the priestly role of Christ. Note how the writer of Hebrews talks about the unique way in which Christ serves us—taking on both the role of priest as well as the role of sacrifice. No one else could have done that for us. His work as the master and means of our salvation explains why His death was like no other and underscores the power of Christ's Resurrection as the confirmation that He is the ultimate High Priest in the order of Melchizedek.

When God speaks to someone, all of history is affected. The Bible describes repeated instances when God spoke directly into an individual's life, and through that person's obedience (and sometimes disobedience) the course of history was altered. Adam, Eve, Cain and Noah have been examples in our study so far. Every book in the Bible represents a moment when God spoke into history through a person to convey His Word—and history was altered.

At the end of Genesis 11, we meet Abram, a man living with his extended family in Haran. God speaks to Abram and gives him a four-part command followed by an amazing set of promises. The command required Abram to (1) go *from* his country, (2) go *from* his kindred, (3) go *from* his father's house and (4) go *to* a land God would show him (Gen. 12:1). He had to leave what he knew and go to what he did not yet know. God invited Abram to leave his old familiar life and start a new life under His guidance. God was working out a plan and also establishing a pattern. This is how God deals with each of us. The Gospel asks us to turn away from the familiar and live by faith in the One who has prepared a place for us that we can't yet see. God promises to be with us on the journey.

"The Gospel asks us to turn away from the familiar and live by faith in the One who has prepared a place for us that we can't yet see. "

As a result of Abram's obedience, God promised him multiplied blessings. In Genesis 12:2–3 God used the words *bless* or *blessing* five times. This is an idea that takes on great importance throughout Genesis and the entire Bible. What does *blessing* mean? One way to understand *blessing* is to describe it as "speaking and delivering good into someone's life." When we say something beneficial, give a good gift or serve another person, we are attempting to bless them. As a result of Abram's obedience, God promised to say and do good in the following ways:

- Abram's offspring would become a great nation.
- Abram himself would experience God's blessing.
- Abram's name would be great.
- Abram would be a blessing to others.

God's command to Abram was limited, but His promises to Abram were unlimited. The children of Abraham (God's updated name for him) have been the recipients of admiration and unusual hatred throughout history. There have been relatively few periods in history when someone hasn't had on their agenda a desire to destroy the Jewish people—think Edom, Moab, Babylon, Persia, Nazi Germany and others even today. And yet they remain. One interesting positive note of Jewish impact is the fact that 12 percent of the Nobel prizes have been awarded to these descendants of Abraham.

Although God has dealt firmly with Israel down through the years, He has also kept that part of His promise concerning those who curse His Chosen People. The nations listed above have suffered extinction or defeat in part because of their treatment of the Jews. That doesn't mean that the Jewish people can do no wrong just because they're God's people. They can be as brutal as any other people can. But there's something about God's promises to His Chosen People of Israel, something that can't be ignored by Bible readers today including you and me.

Abram began his journey well. But he probably wondered at times what God meant by the last part of His promise—"in you all the families of the earth shall be blessed" (Gen. 12:3.) From our vantage point, we realize God was promising the coming of the Messiah, the Savior. And God kept His promise to Abram when He brought Jesus Christ to this earth.

In Genesis 12:7–8 we find that Abram responded with worship and praise. He built an altar in Shechem and another in Bethel. He told all the population around him about the wonderful God that he served.

We find later that circumstances introduce Abram to someone who understood the uniqueness of the God who was leading him—Melchizedek (14:17–20; see also Heb. 7). This "king of Salem" and "priest of the Most High God" declared a blessing on Abram that the patriarch accepted as from God. This time, instead of an altar in recognition of God's faithfulness, Abram gave Melchizedek a tenth of the spoils from his recent victory. The Bible sees in Melchizedek a foreshadowing of Christ—God building into history evidence of His plan for mankind. Abram is the patriarch of God's people and as such was a significant participant in God's painstaking efforts to deliver His creation from slavery to sin. Through Abram, God began to set the cultural stage for Christ.

Express It

God has made promises to you and me. Have you started or are you continuing your journey well with the promises of God? Are you showing your appreciation to God for His goodness? Are you doing it by thanking Him every day? Are you doing it by learning what He wants in your life from His Word? And then are you being obedient to His will? Are you demonstrating your faith in God, both to Him and to those around you? Talk to God about your awareness of His faithfulness and your need to be more faithful.

Consider It

As you read Genesis 12:1–14:24, consider these questions:

1) How do you understand the word *blessing*?

_____

_____

2) In what ways does it appear that Abram fudged a little in doing exactly what God asked him to do? (Check 12:4–5.)

_____

_____

3) What happens between Abram and Lot in these chapters that may have caused Abram to wonder why he allowed Lot to journey with him?

_____

_____

4) How is the episode in Egypt (12:10–20) an example of Abram's humanity and God's faithfulness?

_____

_____

5) What do we learn about Sodom and Gomorrah in these chapters, years before God sealed their fate?

_____

_____

6) Compare Abram's dealings with Melchizedek, the King of Salem (14:18–20), with the King of Sodom (14:21–24).

_____

_____

7) All in all, what have we learned about Abram's character and faith in these three chapters?

_____

_____

God Makes a Covenant

Covenant is one of those words with an uncanny aura of weight. The word seems important. It looks and sounds like a word we should understand and honor. When we do, we discover that a covenant is a gracious undertaking entered into by God for the benefit of those who receive His covenant.

Read Genesis 15:1–18:15

Genesis 15:1–17:14

God's Covenant with Abram

15 After these things the word of the LORD came to Abram in a vision: "Fear not, Abram, I am your shield; your reward shall be very great." ²But Abram said, "O Lord GOD, what will you give me, for I continue childless, and the heir of my house is Eliezer of Damascus?" ³And Abram said, "Behold, you have given me no offspring, and a member of my household will be my heir." ⁴And behold, the word of the LORD came to him: "This man shall not be your heir; your very own son shall be your heir." ⁵And he brought him outside and said, "Look toward heaven, and number the stars, if you are able to number them." Then he said to him, "So shall your offspring be." ⁶And he believed the LORD, and he counted it to him as righteousness.

⁷And he said to him, "I am the LORD who brought you out from Ur of the Chaldeans to give you this land to possess." ⁸But he said, "O Lord GOD, how am I to know that I shall possess it?" ⁹He said to him, "Bring me a heifer three years old, a female goat three years old, a ram three years old, a turtledove, and a young pigeon." ¹⁰And he brought him all these, cut them in half, and laid each half over against the other. But he did not cut the birds in half. ¹¹And when birds of prey came down on the carcasses, Abram drove them away.

¹²As the sun was going down, a deep sleep fell on Abram. And behold, dreadful and great darkness fell upon him. ¹³Then the LORD said to Abram, "Know for certain that your offspring will be sojourners in a land that is not theirs and will be servants there, and they will be afflicted for four hundred years. ¹⁴But I will bring judgment on the nation that they serve, and afterward they shall come out with great possessions. ¹⁵As for yourself, you shall go to your fathers in

> # Key Verse
>
> *On that day the LORD made a covenant with Abram, saying, "To your offspring I give this land, from the river of Egypt to the great river, the river Euphrates"* (Gen. 15:18).

peace; you shall be buried in a good old age. ¹⁶And they shall come back here in the fourth generation, for the iniquity of the Amorites is not yet complete."

¹⁷When the sun had gone down and it was dark, behold, a smoking fire pot and a flaming torch passed between these pieces. ¹⁸On that day the LORD made a covenant with Abram, saying, "To your offspring I give this land, from the river of Egypt to the great river, the river Euphrates, ¹⁹the land of the Kenites, the Kenizzites, the Kadmonites, ²⁰the Hittites, the Perizzites, the Rephaim, ²¹the Amorites, the Canaanites, the Girgashites and the Jebusites."

Sarai and Hagar

16 Now Sarai, Abram's wife, had borne him no children. She had a female Egyptian servant whose name was Hagar. ²And Sarai said to Abram, "Behold now, the LORD has prevented me from bearing children. Go in to my servant; it may be that I shall obtain children by her." And Abram listened to the voice of Sarai. ³So, after Abram had lived ten years in the land of Canaan, Sarai, Abram's wife, took Hagar the Egyptian, her servant, and gave her to Abram her husband as a wife. ⁴And he went in to Hagar, and she conceived. And when she saw that she had conceived, she looked with contempt on her mistress.

⁵And Sarai said to Abram, "May the wrong done to me be on you! I gave my servant to your embrace, and when she saw that she had conceived, she looked on me with contempt. May the Lord judge between you and me!" ⁶But Abram said to Sarai, "Behold, your servant is in your power; do to her as you please." Then Sarai dealt harshly with her, and she fled from her.

⁷The angel of the Lord found her by a spring of water in the wilderness, the spring on the way to Shur. ⁸And he said, "Hagar, servant of Sarai, where have you come from and where are you going?" She said, "I am fleeing from my mistress Sarai." ⁹The angel of the Lord said to her, "Return to your mistress and submit to her." ¹⁰The angel of the Lord also said to her, "I will surely multiply your offspring so that they cannot be numbered for multitude." ¹¹And the angel of the Lord said to her,

> "Behold, you are pregnant
>   and shall bear a son.
> You shall call his name Ishmael,
>   because the Lord has listened
>   to your affliction.
> ¹²He shall be a wild donkey of a man,
>   his hand against everyone
>   and everyone's hand against him,
> and he shall dwell over against all
>   his kinsmen."

¹³So she called the name of the Lord who spoke to her, "You are a God of seeing," for she said, "Truly here I have seen him who looks after me." ¹⁴Therefore the well was called Beerlahairoi; it lies between Kadesh and Bered.

¹⁵And Hagar bore Abram a son, and Abram called the name of his son, whom Hagar bore, Ishmael. ¹⁶Abram was eighty-six years old when Hagar bore Ishmael to Abram.

Abraham and the Covenant of Circumcision

17 When Abram was ninety-nine years old the Lord appeared to Abram and said to him, "I am God Almighty; walk before me, and be blameless, ²that I may make my covenant between me and you, and may multiply you greatly." ³Then Abram fell on his face. And God said to him, ⁴"Behold, my covenant is with you, and you shall be the father of a multitude of nations. ⁵No longer shall your name be called Abram, but your name shall be Abraham, for I have made you the father of a multitude of nations. ⁶I will make you exceedingly fruitful, and I will make you into nations, and kings shall come from you. ⁷And I will establish my covenant between me and you and your offspring after you throughout their generations for an everlasting covenant, to be God to you and to your offspring after you. ⁸And I will give to you and to your offspring after you the land of your sojournings, all the land of Canaan, for an everlasting possession, and I will be their God."

⁹And God said to Abraham, "As for you, you shall keep my covenant, you and your offspring after you throughout their generations. ¹⁰This is my covenant, which you shall keep, between me and you and your offspring after you: Every male among you shall be circumcised. ¹¹You shall be circumcised in the flesh of your foreskins, and it shall be a sign of the covenant between me and you. ¹²He who is eight days old among you shall be circumcised. Every male throughout your generations, whether born in your house or bought with your money from any foreigner who is not of your offspring, ¹³both he who is born in your house and he who is bought with your money, shall surely be circumcised. So shall my covenant be in your flesh an everlasting covenant. ¹⁴Any uncircumcised male who is not circumcised in the flesh of his foreskin shall be cut off from his people; he has broken my covenant."

Go Deeper

If we want a biblical summary of Abraham's character and faith, we need go no further than Genesis 15:6: "And he believed the LORD, and he counted it to him as righteousness." That phrase gets repeated later in Scripture by both Paul and James when they are establishing the nature of faith as the basis of our relationship with God.

Paul talks about faith as the basis of God's dealing with us in Romans 4:1–25 and Galatians 3:1–9. James uses the same description of Abraham to discuss the way genuine faith expresses itself. It's not just a claim; it's a way of living. (See James 2:14–26.)

While a superficial reading of Paul and James has led some people to conclude there's a contradiction between these two biblical writers, what they actually accomplish is to disarm a dual tendency among people: (1) to profess a faith that doesn't make any difference in their lives (the kind of "faith" that's dead without works) or (2) to fail to anchor their faith in God's grace and work but instead place their "faith" in their capacity to please God (the kind of faith that's dead because it rests on human works).

A bram was a man of faith, but he was also a practical man. He believed God had made certain promises to him, but they were tied to his children—and at over 80 years old, Abram didn't expect to have any children, at least by his wife, Sarai. It wasn't that he doubted God's promise; he simply wondered if he needed to do something to "help" God with the problem of Sarai's infertility. When they were younger, their failure to conceive had been a difficulty; but with Abram on the way to his ninetieth birthday and Sarai only a decade behind, the difficulty had become an apparent impossibility. Abram still had to learn, like we all do, that faith deals in impracticalities and impossibilities!

First, Abram tried an alternate explanation as a way to understand God's promise (Gen. 15:1–4). Perhaps God had meant that his wise servant Eliezer was what God had meant when He promised a lasting heritage. Eliezer was like a son and would inherit Abram's estate if a son was not born. God's response was, "This man shall not be your heir; your very own son shall be your heir" (15:4). God then gave Abram a vivid illustration that convinced him in a way that makes Abram "exhibit A" of Old Testament faith: "And he brought

> ## "*Abram . . . had to learn, like we all do, that faith deals in impracticalities and impossibilities!*"

him outside and said, 'Look toward heaven, and number the stars, if you are able to number them.' Then he said to him, 'So shall your offspring be.' And he believed the Lord, and he counted it to him as righteousness" (vv. 5–6).

Abram's recognition that his future was in God's hands was a step of faithful righteousness, and God took note. God responded with a promise, a prophecy and a covenant. The promise involved both a living heritage through a son but also a physical heritage through the land. Next God prophesied to Abram that his offspring would be severely tested by slavery (vv. 13–16). This prophecy was clearly fulfilled by Israel's experience in Egypt. Then God used the animals Abram had sacrificed (vv. 9–11) as a formal way to seal the covenant or agreement between Him and Abram, describing the boundaries of the Promised Land as "from the river of Egypt to the great river, the river Euphrates" (v. 18). Walking between the halves of sacrificed animals was a traditional ceremony that governments of the time used to create a treaty or binding agreement.

Convinced that God planned to give him a son, Abram's second attempt to "help" God came when Sarai suggested that they use a surrogate mom to create a son (Gen. 16). The episode with Hagar and her son Ishmael created a branch in the Abrahamic family (the Arab line) that remains in terrible tension with the chosen seed through Abram and Sarai (the Jewish line). Yet God kept part of His promise to Abram through Hagar's son. That's what the promises of Genesis 16:11–12 mean. Hagar recognized that the God of Abram is the powerful God who spoke to her—the One who saved her life. Notice what she called Him: "So she called the name of the Lord who spoke to her, 'You are a God of seeing,' for she said, 'Truly here I have seen him who looks after me'" (v. 13). How ironic that the mother of the

Arab peoples, who are largely Muslim today, recognized the power and the grace of the God of the Jews!

Thirteen years after Abram and Sarai's botched attempt to assist God's covenant through Ishmael's birth, God renewed His covenant with Abram, changing his name to Abraham (17:5), stating again the benefits (vv. 6–8) and establishing a sign of the covenant—circumcision of males (vv. 10–14). Abraham was now 99 years old. God also changed Sarai's name to Sarah (v. 15) and again told Abraham she would bear him a son. The idea struck Abraham as not only impossible but also funny. He was again being pragmatic, reminding God that his wife was not only infertile, she was also 90 years old! So, he laughed to himself and suggested Ishmael again as a reasonable solution. God heard the laughter but stated again that His everlasting covenant would carry through to Isaac (whose name means "he laughs"), a son who would be born to Abraham and Sarah.

Not long after Abraham and his entire household (including Ishmael) were circumcised, God again visited Abraham. This time Sarah had a chance to hear for herself the Lord's promise of a son within a year's time. She listened from the tent, and like Abraham she laughed. But her laughter was just plain doubt in God, and she confirmed it when she denied she had laughed. God's question hung in the air: "Is anything too hard for the LORD?"(18:14). Sarah thought some things were. Yet God demonstrated to her and Abraham that when He establishes a covenant, no obstacle, even feeble attempts by humans to help Him, will prevent Him from carrying out what He has promised.

Express It

Someone has lamented the fact that too many Christians live like practical agnostics. We regularly doubt God's willingness or even ability to keep His promises. We think we have to explain His "failures" or make excuses for His apparent lack of action. As you pray today, examine how your approach to daily issues reflects your deepest attitudes about God. Talk to Him about what you discover.

Consider It

As you read Genesis 15:1–18:15, consider these questions:

1) How did God emphasize His covenant with Abram?

_____

_____

_____

2) In what ways were Abram's efforts to "help" God actually misapplied faith?

_____

_____

_____

3) In the episode with Hagar, all three adults (Abram, Sarai and Hagar) made mistakes. Describe the lesson God taught each of them.

_____

_____

_____

4) How was God's promise complicated but not derailed by Abram and Sarai's plan involving Hagar and Ishmael?

_____

_____

_____

5) When have you been tempted to compensate for or assist a situation in which it appeared God wasn't keeping His promises?

_____

_____

_____

6) What were the results of your efforts or explanations?

_____

_____

_____

7) How do you typically answer God's question, "Is anything too hard for the LORD"?

_____

_____

_____

Sin Cities

Sodom and Gomorrah may be right at the top of the list of "Unusually Evil Cities That No Longer Exist." Most people have a vague idea how they got on that list. But it's time to get the full story.

Read Genesis 18:1–19:38

18 ¹⁶Then the men set out from there, and they looked down toward Sodom. And Abraham went with them to set them on their way. ¹⁷The LORD said, "Shall I hide from Abraham what I am about to do, ¹⁸seeing that Abraham shall surely become a great and mighty nation, and all the nations of the earth shall be blessed in him? ¹⁹For I have chosen him, that he may command his children and his household after him to keep the way of the LORD by doing righteousness and justice, so that the LORD may bring to Abraham what he has promised him." ²⁰Then the LORD said, "Because the outcry against Sodom and Gomorrah is great and their sin is very grave, ²¹I will go down to see whether they have done altogether according to the outcry that has come to me. And if not, I will know."

Abraham Intercedes for Sodom

²²So the men turned from there and went toward Sodom, but Abraham still stood before the LORD. ²³Then Abraham drew near and said, "Will you indeed sweep away the righteous with the wicked? ²⁴Suppose there are fifty righteous within the city. Will you then sweep away the place and not spare it for the fifty righteous who are in it? ²⁵Far be it from you to do such a thing, to put the righteous to death with the wicked, so that the righteous fare as the wicked! Far be that from you! Shall not the Judge of all the earth do what is just?" ²⁶And the Lord said, "If I find at Sodom fifty righteous in the city, I will spare the whole place for their sake."

²⁷Abraham answered and said, "Behold, I have undertaken to speak to the LORD, I who am but dust and ashes. ²⁸Suppose five of the fifty righteous are lacking. Will you destroy the whole city for lack of five?" And he said, "I will not destroy it if I find forty-five there."

Key Verse

So it was that, when God destroyed the cities of the valley, God remembered Abraham and sent Lot out of the midst of the overthrow when he overthrew the cities in which Lot had lived (Gen. 19:29).

²⁹Again he spoke to him and said, "Suppose forty are found there." He answered, "For the sake of forty I will not do it." ³⁰Then he said, "Oh let not the Lord be angry, and I will speak. Suppose thirty are found there." He answered, "I will not do it, if I find thirty there." ³¹He said, "Behold, I have undertaken to speak to the Lord. Suppose twenty are found there." He answered, "For the sake of twenty I will not destroy it." ³²Then he said, "Oh let not the Lord be angry, and I will speak again but this once. Suppose ten are found there." He answered, "For the sake of ten I will not destroy it." ³³And the LORD went his way, when he had finished speaking to Abraham, and Abraham returned to his place.

God Rescues Lot

19 The two angels came to Sodom in the evening, and Lot was sitting in the gate of Sodom. When Lot saw them, he rose to meet them and bowed himself with his face to the earth ²and said, "My lords, please turn aside to your servant's house and spend the night and wash your feet. Then you may rise up early and go on your way." They said, "No; we will spend the night in the town square." ³But he pressed them strongly; so they turned aside to him and entered his house. And he made them a feast and baked unleavened bread, and they ate.

4But before they lay down, the men of the city, the men of Sodom, both young and old, all the people to the last man, surrounded the house. 5And they called to Lot, "Where are the men who came to you tonight? Bring them out to us, that we may know them." 6Lot went out to the men at the entrance, shut the door after him, 7and said, "I beg you, my brothers, do not act so wickedly. 8Behold, I have two daughters who have not known any man. Let me bring them out to you, and do to them as you please. Only do nothing to these men, for they have come under the shelter of my roof." 9But they said, "Stand back!" And they said, "This fellow came to sojourn, and he has become the judge! Now we will deal worse with you than with them." Then they pressed hard against the man Lot, and drew near to break the door down. 10But the men reached out their hands and brought Lot into the house with them and shut the door. 11And they struck with blindness the men who were at the entrance of the house, both small and great, so that they wore themselves out groping for the door.

12Then the men said to Lot, "Have you anyone else here? Sons-in-law, sons, daughters, or anyone you have in the city, bring them out of the place. 13For we are about to destroy this place, because the outcry against its people has become great before the Lord, and the Lord has sent us to destroy it." 14So Lot went out and said to his sons-in-law, who were to marry his daughters, "Up! Get out of this place, for the Lord is about to destroy the city." But he seemed to his sons-in-law to be jesting.

15As morning dawned, the angels urged Lot, saying, "Up! Take your wife and your two daughters who are here, lest you be swept away in the punishment of the city." 16But he

lingered. So the men seized him and his wife and his two daughters by the hand, the Lord being merciful to him, and they brought him out and set him outside the city. 17And as they brought them out, one said, "Escape for your life. Do not look back or stop anywhere in the valley. Escape to the hills, lest you be swept away." 18And Lot said to them, "Oh, no, my lords. 19Behold, your servant has found favor in your sight, and you have shown me great kindness in saving my life. But I cannot escape to the hills, lest the disaster overtake me and I die. 20Behold, this city is near enough to flee to, and it is a little one. Let me escape there—is it not a little one?—and my life will be saved!" 21He said to him, "Behold, I grant you this favor also, that I will not overthrow the city of which you have spoken. 22Escape there quickly, for I can do nothing till you arrive there." Therefore the name of the city was called Zoar.

God Destroys Sodom

23The sun had risen on the earth when Lot came to Zoar. 24Then the Lord rained on Sodom and Gomorrah sulfur and fire from the Lord out of heaven. 25And he overthrew those cities, and all the valley, and all the inhabitants of the cities, and what grew on the ground. 26But Lot's wife, behind him, looked back, and she became a pillar of salt.

27And Abraham went early in the morning to the place where he had stood before the Lord. 28And he looked down toward Sodom and Gomorrah and toward all the land of the valley, and he looked and, behold, the smoke of the land went up like the smoke of a furnace.

29So it was that, when God destroyed the cities of the valley, God remembered Abraham and sent Lot out of the midst of the overthrow when he overthrew the cities in which Lot had lived.

Lot and His Daughters

³⁰Now Lot went up out of Zoar and lived in the hills with his two daughters, for he was afraid to live in Zoar. So he lived in a cave with his two daughters. ³¹And the firstborn said to the younger, "Our father is old, and there is not a man on earth to come in to us after the manner of all the earth. ³²Come, let us make our father drink wine, and we will lie with him, that we may preserve offspring from our father." ³³So they made their father drink wine that night. And the firstborn went in and lay with her father. He did not know when she lay down or when she arose.

³⁴The next day, the firstborn said to the younger, "Behold, I lay last night with my father. Let us make him drink wine tonight also. Then you go in and lie with him, that we may preserve offspring from our father." ³⁵So they made their father drink wine that night also. And the younger arose and lay with him, and he did not know when she lay down or when she arose. ³⁶Thus both the daughters of Lot became pregnant by their father. ³⁷The firstborn bore a son and called his name Moab. He is the father of the Moabites to this day. ³⁸The younger also bore a son and called his name Ben-ammi. He is the father of the Ammonites to this day.

Go Deeper

In many areas of society today there's an aggressive agenda to affirm and encourage homosexual behavior. But the picture that the Bible presents of homosexuality is consistently negative. Homosexual activity is condemned everywhere in Scripture. It's said to be a wicked act, done by perverted people. Among the earliest laws God gave to His people were prohibitions of sexual acts between members of the same gender (Lev. 18:22; 20:13). A shameful story similar to Lot's is recorded in Judges 19–20.

Passages in the New Testament like Romans 1:26–32 and 1 Corinthians 6:9–11 present a firm and balanced view of sin that includes homosexuality.

The Bible does not focus exclusively on homosexuality as the only way in which humans violate God's gift of sex. Adultery, pornography and other forms of immorality also show profound disregard for God's guidelines for righteous living.

People frequently dismiss Lot's story as an example of hatred and bigotry in Old Testament days. Those attitudes were certainly there; but if you read the story carefully, you'll see that it's not those who believe God's Word who are showing the hatred. Those enamored with sin will stop at nothing to get their way. Sin frequently tries to masquerade as innocence.

Some family members have a knack for getting into trouble. When Abraham allowed his nephew, Lot, to accompany him when he left Haran, he probably had no idea what a continual series of complications the younger man would bring into his life.

Both Lot and Abraham were so prosperous that soon the patriarch had to face the fact that they couldn't live together (Gen. 13:5–18). When he gave Lot first choice of a place to settle, Lot immediately decided on the lush valley of Jordan. An inkling of future trouble can be seen in Genesis 13:13 by the note, "Now the men of Sodom were wicked, great sinners against the LORD."

Soon Lot was caught up in local strife and skirmishes, ending up as a captive of a victorious coalition. Abraham mounted a successful rescue. But Lot returned home to life among the people of Sodom.

During the same visit to Abraham's camp by the oaks of Mamre (18:1), when God told him he would become a father within a year, the Lord also told Abraham He was on an inspection tour of Sodom and Gomorrah to confirm the depth of their depravity, "because the outcry against Sodom and Gomorrah is great and their sin is very grave" (v. 20). Contrary to a lot of current propaganda about victimless sin, there's no such thing as private sin. Sin always affects the sinner and others. God heard from *someone*—those who were suffering because of the rampant sinfulness of those cities. And He intended to take action.

Abraham decided to haggle with God over the fate of the cities (vv. 22–33). He assumed there *must* be some "good" people in the cities. (He knew Lot was there.) So, he probed God's willingness to spare the cities starting with, "Will you then sweep away the place and not spare it for the fifty righteous who are in it?" (v. 24). Abraham "worked" God down to sparing the cities for the sake of ten righteous people (v. 32). God was willing; Sodom and Gomorrah were not.

Genesis 19 opens with Lot sitting as an influential man in the city gate. By now he had been living almost a quarter of a century in Sodom. Apparently, Lot was still a righteous person. But there weren't enough others like him to preserve the city. So, God decided to rescue Lot instead. In fact, 2 Peter 2:6–8 mentions several things about Lot that Genesis doesn't tell us:

> " *The effects of our choices can indeed haunt generations that follow us. And yet through it all, God will remain faithful and work out His plan for the world.* "

If by turning the cities of Sodom and Gomorrah to ashes he condemned them to extinction, making them an example of what is going to happen to the ungodly; and if he rescued righteous Lot, greatly distressed by the sensual conduct of the wicked (for as that righteous man lived among them day after day, he was tormenting his righteous soul over their lawless deeds that he saw and heard).

Obviously, Lot attempted to influence the people of Sodom. Lot didn't agree with the sins of those cities, and he felt terrible about them. But he wasn't bothered enough to take his family out of that cesspool. He was a wealthy man. He enjoyed the honor of being a businessman and a community leader; there's evidence in this story that Sodom may have changed Lot, but Lot never changed Sodom. A good apple never changes the rotten apples in the barrel into good. But the rotten apples can sure change a good apple into bad.

Lot met the Lord's two traveling companions and begged them to come and stay the night with him. He knew what happened to strangers at night in Sodom. Once the men came under his roof, Lot was bound by rules of hospitality. He had to protect them. But the men of Sodom had only one thing on their minds. They wanted to gang rape these strangers. Lot tried to reason with the men and said, "My brothers, do not act so wickedly." His choice of words tells it all.

First, he called them brothers, indicating he felt bound to them. Then he called what they wanted to do "wicked." It's not just a personal preference. It's not their right. It's not something they were born to do. Lot said, "Do not act so wickedly." The Hebrew word that is used here is the word *ra'a'*. It's one of the many Hebrew words for the kind of activity that God will never tolerate.

Lot's words had no effect. The fate of the cities was sealed. God's servants practically had to drag Lot and his family out of harm's way. But the hold of the city was so strong on Lot's wife that she looked back and became a pillar of salt. The effects of the wicked cities stayed with Lot's daughters, and they resorted to incest with their father in the months to come. The two sons fathered this way produced the people called Moabites and Ammonites, perpetual enemies of Abraham's offspring, the Jews.

The effects of our choices can indeed haunt generations that follow us. And yet through it all, God will remain faithful and work out His plan for the world.

Express It

As you pray, consider how you are shaping your life—place that you live, church where you worship, where you are employed—as expressions of your desire to please and serve God. Ask Him for wisdom to honestly evaluate these parts of your relationship with Him and for the courage to make necessary changes.

Consider It

As you read Genesis 18:16–19:38, consider these questions:

1) Why did God decide to tell Abraham about the impending destruction of Sodom and Gomorrah? (See 18:16–21.)

\
\
\

2) What did God's willingness to barter reveal about Him?

\
\
\

3) How was Lot's treatment of the people in Sodom distinctly different from the way those people treated him?

\
\
\

4) What do the actions of Lot's two daughters after their escape tell you about the spiritual state of the family?

\
\
\

5) How does Lot's behavior even during his rapid departure from the city indicate that he didn't grasp what was going on around him? (See 19:17–22.)

\
\
\

6) Why did God engineer Lot's escape from Sodom?

\
\
\

7) What principles about a family living environment can you draw from Lot's time in Sodom?

\
\
\

Lesson
7

On the Way to Fatherhood

Someone said, "Experience is a great thing; it helps us recognize our mistakes when we make them . . . again." We're supposed to learn from our mistakes. But, as Abraham reminds us in these episodes, the lessons are not always remembered.

Read Genesis 20:1–21:34

Abraham and Abimelech

20 From there Abraham journeyed toward the territory of the Negeb and lived between Kadesh and Shur; and he sojourned in Gerar. ²And Abraham said of Sarah his wife, "She is my sister." And Abimelech king of Gerar sent and took Sarah. ³But God came to Abimelech in a dream by night and said to him, "Behold, you are a dead man because of the woman whom you have taken, for she is a man's wife." ⁴Now Abimelech had not approached her. So he said, "Lord, will you kill an innocent people? ⁵Did he not himself say to me, 'She is my sister'? And she herself said, 'He is my brother.' In the integrity of my heart and the innocence of my hands I have done this." ⁶Then God said to him in the dream, "Yes, I know that you have done this in the integrity of your heart, and it was I who kept you from sinning against me. Therefore I did not let you touch her. ⁷Now then, return the man's wife, for he is a prophet, so that he will pray for you, and you shall live. But if you do not return her, know that you shall surely die, you and all who are yours."

⁸So Abimelech rose early in the morning and called all his servants and told them all these things. And the men were very much afraid. ⁹Then Abimelech called Abraham and said to him, "What have you done to us? And how have I sinned against you, that you have brought on me and my kingdom a great sin? You have done to me things that ought not to be done." ¹⁰And Abimelech said to Abraham, "What did you see, that you did this thing?" ¹¹Abraham said, "I did it because I thought, There is no fear of God at all in this place, and they will kill me because of my wife. ¹²Besides, she is indeed my sister, the daughter of my father though not the daughter of my mother, and she became my wife. ¹³And

> # Key Verse
> *And Sarah conceived and bore Abraham a son in his old age at the time of which God had spoken to him* (Gen. 21:2).

when God caused me to wander from my father's house, I said to her, 'This is the kindness you must do me: at every place to which we come, say of me, He is my brother.'"

¹⁴Then Abimelech took sheep and oxen, and male servants and female servants, and gave them to Abraham, and returned Sarah his wife to him. ¹⁵And Abimelech said, "Behold, my land is before you; dwell where it pleases you." ¹⁶To Sarah he said, "Behold, I have given your brother a thousand pieces of silver. It is a sign of your innocence in the eyes of all who are with you, and before everyone you are vindicated." ¹⁷Then Abraham prayed to God, and God healed Abimelech, and also healed his wife and female slaves so that they bore children. ¹⁸For the Lord had closed all the wombs of the house of Abimelech because of Sarah, Abraham's wife.

The Birth of Isaac

21 The Lord visited Sarah as he had said, and the Lord did to Sarah as he had promised. ²And Sarah conceived and bore Abraham a son in his old age at the time of which God had spoken to him. ³Abraham called the name of his son who was born to him, whom Sarah bore him, Isaac. ⁴And Abraham circumcised his son Isaac when he was eight days old, as God had commanded him. ⁵Abraham was a hundred years old when his son Isaac was born to him. ⁶And Sarah said, "God has made laughter for me; everyone who hears will laugh over me." ⁷And she said, "Who would have said to Abraham that Sarah would nurse children? Yet I have borne him a son in his old age."

God Protects Hagar and Ishmael

⁸And the child grew and was weaned. And Abraham made a great feast on the day that Isaac was weaned. ⁹But Sarah saw the son of Hagar the Egyptian, whom she had borne to Abraham, laughing. ¹⁰So she said to Abraham, "Cast out this slave woman with her son, for the son of this slave woman shall not be heir with my son Isaac." ¹¹And the thing was very displeasing to Abraham on account of his son. ¹²But God said to Abraham, "Be not displeased because of the boy and because of your slave woman. Whatever Sarah says to you, do as she tells you, for through Isaac shall your offspring be named. ¹³And I will make a nation of the son of the slave woman also, because he is your offspring." ¹⁴So Abraham rose early in the morning and took bread and a skin of water and gave it to Hagar, putting it on her shoulder, along with the child, and sent her away. And she departed and wandered in the wilderness of Beersheba.

¹⁵When the water in the skin was gone, she put the child under one of the bushes. ¹⁶Then she went and sat down opposite him a good way off, about the distance of a bowshot, for she said, "Let me not look on the death of the child." And as she sat opposite him, she lifted up her voice and wept. ¹⁷And God heard the voice of the boy, and the angel of God called to Hagar from heaven and said to her, "What troubles you, Hagar? Fear not, for God has heard the voice of the boy where he is. ¹⁸Up! Lift up the boy, and hold him fast with your hand, for I will make him into a great nation." ¹⁹Then God opened her eyes, and she saw a well of water. And she went and filled the skin with water and gave the boy a drink. ²⁰And God was with the boy, and he grew up. He lived in the wilderness and became an expert with the bow. ²¹He lived in the wilderness of Paran, and his mother took a wife for him from the land of Egypt.

A Treaty with Abimelech

²²At that time Abimelech and Phicol the commander of his army said to Abraham, "God is with you in all that you do. ²³Now therefore swear to me here by God that you will not deal falsely with me or with my descendants or with my posterity, but as I have dealt kindly with you, so you will deal with me and with the land where you have sojourned." ²⁴And Abraham said, "I will swear."

²⁵When Abraham reproved Abimelech about a well of water that Abimelech's servants had seized, ²⁶Abimelech said, "I do not know who has done this thing; you did not tell me, and I have not heard of it until today." ²⁷So Abraham took sheep and oxen and gave them to Abimelech, and the two men made a covenant. ²⁸Abraham set seven ewe lambs of the flock apart. ²⁹And Abimelech said to Abraham, "What is the meaning of these seven ewe lambs that you have set apart?" ³⁰He said, "These seven ewe lambs you will take from my hand, that this may be a witness for me that I dug this well." ³¹Therefore that place was called Beersheba, because there both of them swore an oath. ³²So they made a covenant at Beersheba. Then Abimelech and Phicol the commander of his army rose up and returned to the land of the Philistines. ³³Abraham planted a tamarisk tree in Beersheba and called there on the name of the Lord, the Everlasting God. ³⁴And Abraham sojourned many days in the land of the Philistines.

Go Deeper

When Abraham asked Hagar and Ishmael to leave his camp, both could have died in the wilderness. They ran out of water. Thirst would have killed them had God not intervened. God said to Abraham, "Go ahead and let them go because I will take care of them." (See Gen. 21:12–13.) God always keeps His promises.

Previously, God told Hagar, "As for Ishmael, I have heard you; behold, I have blessed him and will make him fruitful and multiply him greatly. He shall father twelve princes, and I will make him into a great nation (Gen. 17:20). Here (Gen. 21:17–21) God repeats this promise because He intends to keep His promises despite the deliberate or sometimes accidental ways we try to derail those promises by our choices.

Ishmael became all that God designed him to be. He lived in the Wilderness of Paran. He became an archer, which means he was a hunter in the wilderness, exactly what the Bible said he would be. His mother took a wife for him from Egypt. Why do you suppose that was the case? Hagar was the Egyptian handmaiden (Gen. 16:1). She probably went back to her own family and got a wife for Ishmael from her clan. Since ethnicity is determined by the mother, Ishmael was not a Jew; he was an Egyptian, the father of the Arab peoples.

Here are some of the key passages in Scripture that highlight Ishmael's impact on his extended family: Genesis 25:9–17; 37:25–28; Judges 6–8; Psalm 83:2–6.

R eading these two chapters can be a disappointing experience for someone committed to living by God's principles. Abraham shows us that sometimes those without the presence of God's Spirit act with more integrity than those who have His divine Presence. That is a painful indictment on the lifestyle and the actions of some Christians even today.

Back in Genesis 12, Abraham tried to deceive Pharaoh, the king of Egypt, by calling Sarah his sister. Years later, he tried the same tactic with Abimelech the king of Gerar. Each time he put his wife's life in danger. Apparently Abraham didn't learn from that earlier mistake.

Even in her old age Sarah must have been a "looker" because she got Abimelech's attention. It wasn't long before Abimelech decided to make Abraham's "sister" one of his wives. But before he could complete the arrangement, God got the pagan king's attention. God gave Abimelech an opportunity to preserve his integrity. The word *integrity* here means "wholeness or innocence." Abimelech claimed he acted purely "in the integrity of my heart and the innocence of my hands" (Gen. 20:5). Even the unbeliever can be innocent and still not be godly. Here Abimelech was innocent of doing anything to Sarah. That doesn't mean he was a saint. He wasn't a godly person. He was just innocent in this situation. Given a chance, he gladly escaped with his integrity.

Isn't it interesting that this ungodly person considered adultery a sinful offense? Abimelech is a poster child for the power of conscience in an unbeliever. The apostle Paul accurately described him when he wrote, "For when Gentiles, who do not have the law, by nature do what the law requires, they are a law to themselves, even though they do not have the law. They show that the work of the law is written on their hearts, while their conscience also bears witness, and their conflicting thoughts accuse or even excuse them" (Rom. 2:14–15).

Abimelech was able to confront Abraham because the patriarch should have known better! Over and over again in Genesis 20:9–10 he laid the blame at the feet of Abraham. And Abraham did what most of us do: he tried to offer an explanation that was absolutely absurd. (See vv. 11–13.) The one who knew God had a lot to learn from the one who did not yet know God.

Abraham knew that God is greater than any human, Pharaoh or king; but he didn't behave like he knew. The bad guys can't thwart the promises and purposes of God (neither can the good guys). We can trust God to do what is right because He is the sovereign king of the universe, not because we're trustworthy. Abraham and Sarah were certainly far from trustworthy. Yet God accomplished His purposes.

When the people of Israel heard these all-too-human stories, they realized how secure they were as God's people. Nothing could stop His promised blessing or His salvation. What's true for Israel is true for us too. If Abraham and Sarah could make such foolish mistakes and still enjoy the forgiveness and blessing of God, we can too. We should never be recklessly foolish just because we know we can be forgiven. But when we are foolish, we should remember that God's

> ❝*When we are foolish, we should remember that God's plans and promises for our lives can't be destroyed even through our foolishness.*❞

plans and promises for our lives can't be destroyed even through our foolishness.

On the way to parenthood, Abraham and Sarah were repeatedly foolish. Yet in God's timing, Isaac was born. Soon the consequences of a past foolish act reared their ugly heads in the form of Ishmael's mocking Isaac and Sarah's jealousy-fueled efforts to expel Hagar and Ishmael from the household. We can't tell who was more jealous, the teenage Ishmael over Isaac's birth or Sarah over the threat to Isaac she saw in Ishmael. Sarah decided to eliminate the problem. Yet God, for the sake of His promise to Abraham, had decided He would also bless Hagar and her offspring. He directed the thirsty mother and child to a well in the wilderness and saved their lives. But the conflict in the family goes on to this day.

We know every time we pick up a newspaper or every time we look at the television that there are problems in the Middle East. Those problems go right back to the jealousy sparked by foolishness so long ago.

How is it possible for us to defeat the kind of jealousy that can spark generations of hatred and violence? We begin by seeing everything as God's gift. Then we won't be jealous over what our neighbor has because those things are God's gift to him or her, and God has given other gifts to us.

If jealousy is a problem for you, confess it to God and ask for forgiveness. Ask Him to take it away from you just like you would ask Him to take cancer away from you. More people may be destroyed because of jealousy than because of cancer, so don't allow jealousy to take root in your life. Confess it to God, because if you don't get rid of it, if you don't deal with it, you can look into your own future and see the same sort of conflict you read about in Genesis 21.

Express It

This lesson ended with a focus on jealousy—evidence of a lack of contentment with God's faithfulness, protection and supply. Review the last paragraphs of the lesson prayerfully, and ask God to reveal to you areas in which envy may be creating a pattern of distrust, bitterness and unhappiness. Take the spiritual steps to remedy the situation.

Consider It

As you read Genesis 20:1–21:34, consider these questions:

1) How did God demonstrate His compassion for Abimelech when the king added Sarah to his harem?

_____

_____

2) What was Abraham's excuse for calling Sarah his sister?

_____

_____

3) What examples have you noticed where the ungodly have demonstrated more integrity than those who were supposed to be godly?

_____

_____

4) In what ways was Sarah herself the main source of her problems with Hagar and Ishmael?

_____

_____

5) Why did God instruct Abraham to carry out Sarah's demand that Hagar and Ishmael be driven from their home?

_____

_____

6) What did Abimelech ask Abraham to promise when they made a covenant between them?

_____

_____

7) Describe what we learn about God's character in these two chapters of Scripture.

_____

_____

Tested!

What do you do when God asks you to do something that doesn't make sense? What do you do when your responsibility runs in the opposite direction of your understanding—when sensibility challenges responsibility? Abraham shows us how difficult a challenge this can be.

Read Genesis 22:1–24

The Sacrifice of Isaac

22 After these things God tested Abraham and said to him, "Abraham!" And he said, "Here am I." ²He said, "Take your son, your only son Isaac, whom you love, and go to the land of Moriah, and offer him there as a burnt offering on one of the mountains of which I shall tell you." ³So Abraham rose early in the morning, saddled his donkey, and took two of his young men with him, and his son Isaac. And he cut the wood for the burnt offering and arose and went to the place of which God had told him. ⁴On the third day Abraham lifted up his eyes and saw the place from afar. ⁵Then Abraham said to his young men, "Stay here with the donkey; I and the boy will go over there and worship and come again to you." ⁶And Abraham took the wood of the burnt offering and laid it on Isaac his son. And he took in his hand the fire and the knife. So they went both of them together. ⁷And Isaac said to his father Abraham, "My father!" And he said, "Here am I, my son." He said, "Behold, the fire and the wood, but where is the lamb for a burnt offering?" ⁸Abraham said, "God will provide for himself the lamb for a burnt offering, my son." So they went both of them together.

⁹When they came to the place of which God had told him, Abraham built the altar there and laid the wood in order and bound Isaac his son and laid him on the altar, on top of the wood. ¹⁰Then Abraham reached out his hand and took the knife to slaughter his son. ¹¹But the angel of the LORD called to him from heaven and said, "Abraham, Abraham!" And he said, "Here am I." ¹²He said, "Do not lay your hand on the boy or do anything to him, for now I know that you fear God, seeing you have not withheld your son, your only son, from me." ¹³And Abraham lifted up his eyes and looked, and behold, behind him was a ram,

> # Key Verse
>
> He said, "Take your son, your only son Isaac, whom you love, and go to the land of Moriah, and offer him there as a burnt offering on one of the mountains of which I shall tell you" (Gen. 22:2).

caught in a thicket by his horns. And Abraham went and took the ram and offered it up as a burnt offering instead of his son. ¹⁴So Abraham called the name of that place, "The LORD will provide"; as it is said to this day, "On the mount of the LORD it shall be provided."

¹⁵And the angel of the LORD called to Abraham a second time from heaven ¹⁶and said, "By myself I have sworn, declares the LORD, because you have done this and have not withheld your son, your only son, ¹⁷I will surely bless you, and I will surely multiply your offspring as the stars of heaven and as the sand that is on the seashore. And your offspring shall possess the gate of his enemies, ¹⁸and in your offspring shall all the nations of the earth be blessed, because you have obeyed my voice." ¹⁹So Abraham returned to his young men, and they arose and went together to Beersheba. And Abraham lived at Beersheba.

²⁰Now after these things it was told to Abraham, "Behold, Milcah also has borne children to your brother Nahor: ²¹Uz his firstborn, Buz his brother, Kemuel the father of Aram, ²²Chesed, Hazo, Pildash, Jidlaph, and Bethuel." ²³(Bethuel fathered Rebekah.) These eight Milcah bore to Nahor, Abraham's brother. ²⁴Moreover, his concubine, whose name was Reumah, bore Tebah, Gaham, Tahash, and Maacah.

Go Deeper

Every time God revealed Himself to Abraham, the patriarch progressed in his fellowship with and his understanding of God. Many times when God revealed Himself to Abraham, the results were a test. The same process happens with us today, except we meet God in His Word and not in personal appearances. Every time we meet with God in His Word, we have the opportunity to progress in our fellowship with and our understanding of God.

Genesis 12:1–3 records God's first appearance to Abraham. God revealed His discontent with the world's society. He asked Abraham to leave Ur of the Chaldeans and move to a place that He would show him. God promised blessings and expected obedience.

In Genesis 13:14–17 God appeared a second time and revealed His plans and His promises to Abraham. Again, the patriarch was asked to move under God's direction.

In Genesis 15:1–6, the third appearance, God revealed His patience with Abraham because Abraham suggested Eliezer of Damascus might be his heir and God said, "No, I'm going to provide a son for you, your own son."

Again in Genesis 15:7–21, the fourth appearance of God to Abraham, He revealed that He provides hope when things look impossible. God sealed His covenant with Abraham with a sacrifice. God always does that. When we find God in His Word, we find hope in His Word. God's Word assures us, "What then shall we say to these things? If God is for us, who can be against us? He who did not spare his own Son but gave him up for us all, how will he not also with him graciously give us all things?" (Rom. 8:31–32).

In Genesis 17:1–21, the fifth appearance, God revealed His sufficiency to keep His promises. What God promises you, God will perform.

In the sixth appearance in Genesis 18:1–33, God revealed His justice mingled with His mercy in the case of Sodom and Gomorrah.

The seventh time God appeared to Abraham is in our current passage (Gen. 22:1–19). Here God revealed the fellowship of His suffering. After each encounter, Abraham knew God better. After each time you encounter God in His Word, you'll know Him better too.

Genesis 22 begins with an ominous statement: "After these things God tested Abraham and said to him, 'Abraham!' And he said, 'Here am I'" (v. 1). Abraham was about to embark on the patriarch's greatest test of faith. God appeared in order to test the faith of Abraham. As with most of God's encounters with Abraham, the patriarch had to move at God's command.

We instinctively wonder if that's a good idea—being tested by God. Hebrews 11 says, "By faith Abraham, when he was tested, offered up Isaac, and he who had received the promises was in the act of offering up his only son, of whom it was said, 'Through Isaac shall your offspring be named'" (Heb. 11:17–18). The record of this event proves to us that it was a good idea for God to test Abraham, just like it's a good idea for God to test your faith and mine. We don't like that, of course, but after the test has been passed, our faith is always stronger.

This event helps us to understand what was on the mind of James when he wrote, "Was not Abraham our father justified by works when he offered up his son Isaac on the altar? You see that faith was active along with his works, and faith was completed by his works" (James 2:21–22). James's comments here have initiated a lot of controversy over the years, but his point is that faith that doesn't stand up to God's test really isn't faith at all.

Faith that doesn't produce a life of godliness isn't the kind of faith that can save us. James isn't saying that you have to add works to your faith. We're saved by faith plus nothing else. But the kind of faith that saves is not the kind of faith that just talks about it. It's the kind of faith that proves itself in action. Was it right for God to test Abraham? Is it right for God to test your faith today? If our faith isn't tried and tested, how do we know it's true?

God tested Job's faith, Peter's faith and Philip's faith. God seems to be saying, "The untested faith isn't worth having." Testing your faith only makes it stronger. When God comes to test your faith, you can step up to the plate just like Abraham did.

God set Abraham's responsibility on a collision course with his sensibility. Genesis 22:2 says, "Take your son, your only son Isaac,

"Is it right for God to test your faith today? If our faith isn't tried and tested, how do we know it's true?"

whom you love, and go to the land of Moriah, and offer him there as a burnt offering on one of the mountains of which I shall tell you." Think of the impact of God's request: Abraham and Sarah waited for Isaac's birth for *decades*. God had told them He would establish His covenant through their miracle son. Was He now changing His mind?

God told Abraham to go to the land of Moriah and offer Isaac as a burnt offering. Go without hesitation. Go to an undisclosed mountain, one I'll tell you of. This sounds a lot like an earlier "test" (Gen. 12:1), when Abraham first left his homeland.

God often leads us when we don't know where we're going. God leads us when we have faith in Him, and we respond by obedience. Those works say to God, "Lord, I don't have to know where I'm going as long as I know that You are leading me." Our trust doesn't have to be very big as long as it rests in a big God!

God told Abraham to do something that he couldn't possibly understand, but he rose early in the morning and got to it. Abraham had the kind of character that says, "If this is what God wants, I will obey." Abraham went to the place God directed him.

Abraham described the impending sacrifice of his only beloved son as an act of worship to God (22:5). This is the first time the Hebrew word *shachah* (worship) occurs in the Bible. It means "to fall down, bow down, fall prostrate and worship God." It's used more than 150 times in Scripture. It makes an important distinction. Praise is always up in the Bible. Worship is always down. Come let us worship and bow down. That's what Abraham was about to do.

When Abraham was ready to take the life of his covenant son, the angel of the Lord interceded. He told Abraham not to do anything to his son. God did exactly to Isaac what Abraham predicted (Gen. 22:8) though Abraham didn't know the depth of his words. God provided a substitute, something to die in the place of Isaac.

That is exactly what God did for you and me: Jesus Christ went to the cross, not because He was guilty, nor because He was a sinner, nor even because He had done something wrong. In fact, nobody could find something He did wrong. He went to the cross to die in our place. He is our substitute.

Express It

Like tests in school, the tests God brings into our lives aren't intended to cause our failure but to encourage and measure our growth. As you pray, think about the tests God may have recently allowed you to experience. How have you benefited from them? Talk to God about what you've learned about Him as a result of the tests you've experienced.

Consider It

As you read Genesis 22:1–24, consider these questions:

1) What do you think was the meaning of Abraham's answer to God in 22:1?

_____

_____

_____

2) In what situations have you found yourself tested by God? How have you done?

_____

_____

_____

3) What do you think Abraham was thinking and feeling as he prepared for the journey?

_____

_____

_____

4) What parallels can you see between God's conversation with Abraham in 22:1–3 and Abraham's conversations with Isaac in 22:7–8?

_____

_____

_____

5) How would you describe Isaac's participation in this event?

_____

_____

_____

6) What must have been some of Abraham's first thoughts when the angel of the Lord interrupted his act of sacrifice?

_____

_____

_____

7) What was God teaching Abraham by this test?

_____

_____

_____

Lesson
9

Isaac's Wedding

At some point (usually soon after we become parents), we begin to think about becoming parents-in-law. We realize our kids will probably marry. We want them to make good choices. But what would we do if the choice was up to us?

Read Genesis 23:1–25:18
Genesis 24:1–67

Isaac and Rebekah

24 Now Abraham was old, well advanced in years. And the LORD had blessed Abraham in all things. ²And Abraham said to his servant, the oldest of his household, who had charge of all that he had, "Put your hand under my thigh, ³that I may make you swear by the LORD, the God of heaven and God of the earth, that you will not take a wife for my son from the daughters of the Canaanites, among whom I dwell, ⁴but will go to my country and to my kindred, and take a wife for my son Isaac." ⁵The servant said to him, "Perhaps the woman may not be willing to follow me to this land. Must I then take your son back to the land from which you came?" ⁶Abraham said to him, "See to it that you do not take my son back there. ⁷The LORD, the God of heaven, who took me from my father's house and from the land of my kindred, and who spoke to me and swore to me, 'To your offspring I will give this land,' he will send his angel before you, and you shall take a wife for my son from there. ⁸But if the woman is not willing to follow you, then you will be free from this oath of mine; only you must not take my son back there." ⁹So the servant put his hand under the thigh of Abraham his master and swore to him concerning this matter.

¹⁰Then the servant took ten of his master's camels and departed, taking all sorts of choice gifts from his master; and he arose and went to Mesopotamia to the city of Nahor. ¹¹And he made the camels kneel down outside the city by the well of water at the time of evening, the time when women go out to draw water. ¹²And he said, "O LORD, God of my master Abraham, please grant me success today and show steadfast love to my master Abraham. ¹³Behold, I am standing by the spring of water, and the

Key Verse

"Blessed be the LORD, the God of my master Abraham, who has not forsaken his steadfast love and his faithfulness toward my master. As for me, the LORD has led me in the way to the house of my master's kinsmen" (Gen. 24:27).

daughters of the men of the city are coming out to draw water. ¹⁴Let the young woman to whom I shall say, 'Please let down your jar that I may drink,' and who shall say, 'Drink, and I will water your camels'—let her be the one whom you have appointed for your servant Isaac. By this I shall know that you have shown steadfast love to my master."

¹⁵Before he had finished speaking, behold, Rebekah, who was born to Bethuel the son of Milcah, the wife of Nahor, Abraham's brother, came out with her water jar on her shoulder. ¹⁶The young woman was very attractive in appearance, a maiden whom no man had known. She went down to the spring and filled her jar and came up. ¹⁷Then the servant ran to meet her and said, "Please give me a little water to drink from your jar." ¹⁸She said, "Drink, my lord." And she quickly let down her jar upon her hand and gave him a drink. ¹⁹When she had finished giving him a drink, she said, "I will draw water for your camels also, until they have finished drinking." ²⁰So she quickly emptied her jar into the trough and ran again to the well to draw water, and she drew for all his camels. ²¹The man gazed at her in silence to learn

whether the Lord had prospered his journey or not.

²²When the camels had finished drinking, the man took a gold ring weighing a half shekel, and two bracelets for her arms weighing ten gold shekels, ²³and said, "Please tell me whose daughter you are. Is there room in your father's house for us to spend the night?" ²⁴She said to him, "I am the daughter of Bethuel the son of Milcah, whom she bore to Nahor." ²⁵She added, "We have plenty of both straw and fodder, and room to spend the night." ²⁶The man bowed his head and worshiped the Lord ²⁷and said, "Blessed be the Lord, the God of my master Abraham, who has not forsaken his steadfast love and his faithfulness toward my master. As for me, the Lord has led me in the way to the house of my master's kinsmen." ²⁸Then the young woman ran and told her mother's household about these things.

²⁹Rebekah had a brother whose name was Laban. Laban ran out toward the man, to the spring. ³⁰As soon as he saw the ring and the bracelets on his sister's arms, and heard the words of Rebekah his sister, "Thus the man spoke to me," he went to the man. And behold, he was standing by the camels at the spring. ³¹He said, "Come in, O blessed of the Lord. Why do you stand outside? For I have prepared the house and a place for the camels." ³²So the man came to the house and unharnessed the camels, and gave straw and fodder to the camels, and there was water to wash his feet and the feet of the men who were with him. ³³Then food was set before him to eat. But he said, "I will not eat until I have said what I have to say." He said, "Speak on."

³⁴So he said, "I am Abraham's servant. ³⁵The Lord has greatly blessed my master, and he has become great. He has given him flocks and herds, silver and gold, male servants and female servants, camels and donkeys. ³⁶And Sarah my master's wife bore a son to my master when she was old, and to him he has given all that he has. ³⁷My master made me swear, saying, 'You shall not take a wife for my son from the daughters of the Canaanites, in whose land I dwell, ³⁸but you shall go to my father's house and to my clan and take a wife for my son.' ³⁹I said to my master, 'Perhaps the woman will not follow me.' ⁴⁰But he said to me, 'The Lord, before whom I have walked, will send his angel with you and prosper your way. You shall take a wife for my son from my clan and from my father's house. ⁴¹Then you will be free from my oath, when you come to my clan. And if they will not give her to you, you will be free from my oath.'

⁴²"I came today to the spring and said, 'O Lord, the God of my master Abraham, if now you are prospering the way that I go, ⁴³behold, I am standing by the spring of water. Let the virgin who comes out to draw water, to whom I shall say, "Please give me a little water from your jar to drink," ⁴⁴and who will say to me, "Drink, and I will draw for your camels also," let her be the woman whom the Lord has appointed for my master's son.'

⁴⁵"Before I had finished speaking in my heart, behold, Rebekah came out with her water jar on her shoulder, and she went down to the spring and drew water. I said to her, 'Please let me drink.' ⁴⁶She quickly let down her jar from her shoulder and said, 'Drink, and I will give your camels drink also.' So I drank, and she gave the camels drink also. ⁴⁷Then I asked her, 'Whose daughter are you?' She said, 'The daughter of Bethuel, Nahor's son, whom Milcah bore to him.' So I put the ring on her nose and the bracelets on her arms. ⁴⁸Then I bowed my head and worshiped the Lord and blessed the Lord, the God of my master Abraham, who had led me by the right way to take the daughter of my master's kinsman for his son. ⁴⁹Now then, if you are going to show steadfast love and faithfulness to my master, tell me; and if not, tell me, that I may turn to the right hand or to the left."

⁵⁰Then Laban and Bethuel answered and said, "The thing has come from the

LORD; we cannot speak to you bad or good. ⁵¹Behold, Rebekah is before you; take her and go, and let her be the wife of your master's son, as the LORD has spoken."

⁵²When Abraham's servant heard their words, he bowed himself to the earth before the LORD. ⁵³And the servant brought out jewelry of silver and of gold, and garments, and gave them to Rebekah. He also gave to her brother and to her mother costly ornaments. ⁵⁴And he and the men who were with him ate and drank, and they spent the night there. When they arose in the morning, he said, "Send me away to my master." ⁵⁵Her brother and her mother said, "Let the young woman remain with us a while, at least ten days; after that she may go." ⁵⁶But he said to them, "Do not delay me, since the LORD has prospered my way. Send me away that I may go to my master." ⁵⁷They said, "Let us call the young woman and ask her." ⁵⁸And they called Rebekah and said to her, "Will you go with this man?" She said, "I will go." ⁵⁹So they sent away Rebekah their sister and her nurse, and Abraham's servant and his men. ⁶⁰And they blessed Rebekah and said to her,

"Our sister, may you become
    thousands of ten thousands,
and may your offspring possess
    the gate of those who hate him!"

⁶¹Then Rebekah and her young women arose and rode on the camels and followed the man. Thus the servant took Rebekah and went his way.

⁶²Now Isaac had returned from Beer-lahai-roi and was dwelling in the Negeb. ⁶³And Isaac went out to meditate in the field toward evening. And he lifted up his eyes and saw, and behold, there were camels coming. ⁶⁴And Rebekah lifted up her eyes, and when she saw Isaac, she dismounted from the camel ⁶⁵and said to the servant, "Who is that man, walking in the field to meet us?" The servant said, "It is my master." So she took her veil and covered herself. ⁶⁶And the servant told Isaac all the things that he had done. ⁶⁷Then Isaac brought her into the tent of Sarah his mother and took Rebekah, and she became his wife, and he loved her. So Isaac was comforted after his mother's death.

Go Deeper

Although Isaac and Rebekah's marriage was arranged, she had a major impact on the proceedings. Think about how her immediate behavior at the well gave Abraham's servant an instant glimpse into her character. See in particular passages like Genesis 24:18–21, 25, 28, 57–61. How was her response a wise choice, and what does it tell us about her?

We ought to give our children plenty of insight into what kind of mate to look for, but we can't underestimate the value of training our children to be the right kind of mate. One of the challenges faced by young people in today's society is the emphasis on *finding the right one* rather than *becoming the right one*. When the focus is on "whom will I marry," it's also on "who will serve me and meet my needs." But when the focus is on "what kind of marriage mate will I be," it's also on "whom will I serve."

The first impression the servant got of Rebekah was that she was a beautiful woman willing to serve. She didn't use her beauty as an excuse to have others serve her. God took care of a lot of the other details.

Isaac, the miracle child of Abraham and Sarah, was 36 years old when his mother died. Sarah had reached the age of 127. For reasons we're not told, Abraham hadn't yet arranged for a wife for Isaac. But when Sarah died, the patriarch seemed to realize that God's covenant with him required that his only son beget another generation who would benefit from God's faithfulness.

So, Abraham called in a trusted servant and gave him the task of bride-finder. He asked the servant to swear an unusual oath: "Put your hand under my thigh, that I may make you swear by the LORD" (Gen. 24:2–3). The Hebrew word for *thigh* is the word *yarek*. It comes from the root word meaning to "be soft or of soft tissue." It generally refers to the thigh of the leg.

Sometimes this word *yarek* is used to indicate the side of something (Ex. 40:22, Lev. 1:11) or the "leg" of an inanimate object (Ex. 25:31). But here the word seems to have a very special meaning. It's entirely possible that Abraham is asking his oldest servant to grab his leg, the seat of power, the seat of strength, to take an oath while holding onto his leg, much like you and I would shake hands today. But this was the most graphic, the most resolute oath that Abraham could think of. Apparently it was something that may not have existed in the ancient Near East before that time. Abraham created a unique form of oath that made the duty of finding the right mate for Isaac a great and solemn responsibility. Abraham was setting the guidelines for his servant to follow in choosing a mate for his son.

And he made the servant swear an oath that he wouldn't take one of the daughters of the Canaanites, that he would only take for Isaac a wife out of Abraham's own extended family.

Given the task he had been assigned and the trust that it implied, the servant had every right to question whether or not a woman was going to follow a stranger, leave her home and go to a country she had never been to before. Wouldn't it be better to take Isaac along? But Abraham was absolutely adamant that Eliezer was not to take Isaac and that he was to select a wife from Abraham's family (Gen. 24:4–6). So, the servant took the oath; he wouldn't deviate from the divine guidelines that were set by Abraham, no matter what.

"Without God, there is no success. There's no success in marriage without the blessing of God."

Genesis 24:10–14 describes how Abraham's servant prepared to meet Isaac's bride. He gave God plenty of room to operate. He decided on a strategy, and God honored his humble approach.

The servant went to the city where Nahor, the brother of Abraham, lived. He went to the place where it was most likely he would find the right woman. He also parked his camel train by the town well. That's where he would gather information. The local well was the ancient equivalent of an Internet café today.

The wise servant asked God for success. Without God, there is no success. There's no success in marriage without the blessing of God. This servant did all the right things. He devised the test that would reveal the character of the young woman who would come to the well. The servant was worthy of his master.

Now, is there anything we can learn in the twenty-first century from this story of Abraham sending his servant to find a bride for Isaac? Certainly! In fact, we need to follow the same basic procedure. We must always establish divine guidelines before we look for a life's mate. That's a key lesson young people need to learn when they are involved in selecting a marriage partner.

For example, 2 Corinthians 6:14–15 requires believers to marry only those who are part of the family of God: "Do not be unequally yoked with unbelievers. For what partnership has righteousness with lawlessness? Or what fellowship has light with darkness? What accord has Christ with Belial? Or what portion does a believer share with an unbeliever?"

In Abraham's day, this principle of setting divine guidelines ensured that Isaac wouldn't take a wife from the pagan Canaanites who lived all around him. In the twenty-first century this principle is still wise, righteous and godly. Don't seek a mate from the world around you. Seek a mate from within the family of God. That's the only kind of marriage God promises to bless. Let Him bless yours.

Express It

Our passage for this lesson covers two major events in a person's life: the end of a marriage through death and the beginning of another. Grief and happiness are two of the basic ingredients of life. Our capacity to feel and learn from both is a gift from God. Talk to Him about the way you're dealing with the ups and downs of life. To what degree are you allowing Him to affect the mountains and valleys you're journeying through?

Consider It

As you read Genesis 23:1–25:18, consider these questions:

1) How do the arrangements for Sarah's funeral reveal the relationship between Abraham and his neighbors?

_____

_____

_____

2) Why did Abraham insist on paying for the burial site?

_____

_____

_____

3) What are some of the advantages and disadvantages of a system where parents choose their children's marriage partners?

_____

_____

_____

4) How should parents be involved today? Why?

_____

_____

_____

5) Describe the "negotiations" between Abraham's servant and Rebekah's family.

_____

_____

_____

6) What are some of the reasons why Rebekah might have agreed to go back with the servant when given the choice (Gen. 24:57–58)?

_____

_____

_____

7) How does the Bible describe Isaac and Rebekah's first encounter and their early life together?

_____

_____

_____

Jacob and the Blessing

The term siblings *takes on a special significance when it comes to twins. For all their similarities, twins are individuals who have different personalities. No story demonstrates this more clearly than the account of Isaac's twin sons, Jacob and Esau.*

Read Genesis 25:19–27:46

Genesis 25, 27

The Birth of Esau and Jacob

25 ¹⁹These are the generations of Isaac, Abraham's son: Abraham fathered Isaac, ²⁰and Isaac was forty years old when he took Rebekah, the daughter of Bethuel the Aramean of Paddan-aram, the sister of Laban the Aramean, to be his wife. ²¹And Isaac prayed to the LORD for his wife, because she was barren. And the LORD granted his prayer, and Rebekah his wife conceived. ²²The children struggled together within her, and she said, "If it is thus, why is this happening to me?" So she went to inquire of the LORD. ²³And the LORD said to her,

> "Two nations are in your womb,
>   and two peoples from within you
>   shall be divided;
> the one shall be stronger than the
>   other,
>   the older shall serve the younger."

²⁴When her days to give birth were completed, behold, there were twins in her womb. ²⁵The first came out red, all his body like a hairy cloak, so they called his name Esau. ²⁶Afterward his brother came out with his hand holding Esau's heel, so his name was called Jacob. Isaac was sixty years old when she bore them.

²⁷When the boys grew up, Esau was a skillful hunter, a man of the field, while Jacob was a quiet man, dwelling in tents. ²⁸Isaac loved Esau because he ate of his game, but Rebekah loved Jacob.

Esau Sells His Birthright

²⁹Once when Jacob was cooking stew, Esau came in from the field, and he was exhausted. ³⁰And Esau said to Jacob, "Let me eat some of that red stew, for I am exhausted!" (Therefore his name was called Edom.) ³¹Jacob said, "Sell me your birthright now." ³²Esau said, "I am about

Key Verse

And the LORD said to her, "Two nations are in your womb, and two peoples from within you shall be divided; the one shall be stronger than the other, the older shall serve the younger" (Gen. 25:23).

to me?" ³³Jacob said, "Swear to me now." So he swore to him and sold his birthright to Jacob. ³⁴Then Jacob gave Esau bread and lentil stew, and he ate and drank and rose and went his way. Thus Esau despised his birthright.

* * * * * * * * * * * * * * *

Isaac Blesses Jacob

27 When Isaac was old and his eyes were dim so that he could not see, he called Esau his older son and said to him, "My son"; and he answered, "Here I am." ²He said, "Behold, I am old; I do not know the day of my death. ³Now then, take your weapons, your quiver and your bow, and go out to the field and hunt game for me, ⁴and prepare for me delicious food, such as I love, and bring it to me so that I may eat, that my soul may bless you before I die."

⁵Now Rebekah was listening when Isaac spoke to his son Esau. So when Esau went to the field to hunt for game and bring it, ⁶Rebekah said to her son Jacob, "I heard your father speak to your brother Esau, ⁷'Bring me game

and prepare for me delicious food, that I may eat it and bless you before the Lord before I die.' ⁸Now therefore, my son, obey my voice as I command you. ⁹Go to the flock and bring me two good young goats, so that I may prepare from them delicious food for your father, such as he loves. ¹⁰And you shall bring it to your father to eat, so that he may bless you before he dies." ¹¹But Jacob said to Rebekah his mother, "Behold, my brother Esau is a hairy man, and I am a smooth man. ¹²Perhaps my father will feel me, and I shall seem to be mocking him and bring a curse upon myself and not a blessing." ¹³His mother said to him, "Let your curse be on me, my son; only obey my voice, and go, bring them to me."

¹⁴So he went and took them and brought them to his mother, and his mother prepared delicious food, such as his father loved. ¹⁵Then Rebekah took the best garments of Esau her older son, which were with her in the house, and put them on Jacob her younger son. ¹⁶And the skins of the young goats she put on his hands and on the smooth part of his neck. ¹⁷And she put the delicious food and the bread, which she had prepared, into the hand of her son Jacob.

¹⁸So he went in to his father and said, "My father." And he said, "Here I am. Who are you, my son?" ¹⁹Jacob said to his father, "I am Esau your firstborn. I have done as you told me; now sit up and eat of my game, that your soul may bless me." ²⁰But Isaac said to his son, "How is it that you have found it so quickly, my son?" He answered, "Because the Lord your God granted me success." ²¹Then Isaac said to Jacob, "Please come near, that I may feel you, my son, to know whether you are really my son Esau or not." ²²So Jacob went near to Isaac his father, who felt him and said, "The voice is Jacob's voice, but the hands are the hands of Esau." ²³And he did not

recognize him, because his hands were hairy like his brother Esau's hands. So he blessed him. ²⁴He said, "Are you really my son Esau?" He answered, "I am." ²⁵Then he said, "Bring it near to me, that I may eat of my son's game and bless you." So he brought it near to him, and he ate; and he brought him wine, and he drank.

²⁶Then his father Isaac said to him, "Come near and kiss me, my son." ²⁷So he came near and kissed him. And Isaac smelled the smell of his garments and blessed him and said,

> "See, the smell of my son
> is as the smell of a field that the
> Lord has blessed!
> ²⁸ May God give you of the dew of
> heaven
> and of the fatness of the earth
> and plenty of grain and wine.
> ²⁹ Let peoples serve you,
> and nations bow down to you.
> Be lord over your brothers,
> and may your mother's sons bow
> down to you.
> Cursed be everyone who curses
> you,
> and blessed be everyone who
> blesses you!"

³⁰As soon as Isaac had finished blessing Jacob, when Jacob had scarcely gone out from the presence of Isaac his father, Esau his brother came in from his hunting. ³¹He also prepared delicious food and brought it to his father. And he said to his father, "Let my father arise and eat of his son's game, that you may bless me." ³² His father Isaac said to him, "Who are you?" He answered, "I am your son, your firstborn, Esau." ³³Then Isaac trembled very violently and said, "Who was it then that hunted game and brought it to me, and I ate it all before you came, and I have blessed him? Yes, and he shall be blessed." ³⁴As soon as Esau heard the words of his father, he

cried out with an exceedingly great and bitter cry and said to his father, "Bless me, even me also, O my father!" ³⁵ But he said, "Your brother came deceitfully, and he has taken away your blessing." ³⁶Esau said, "Is he not rightly named Jacob? For he has cheated me these two times. He took away my birthright, and behold, now he has taken away my blessing." Then he said, "Have you not reserved a blessing for me?" ³⁷Isaac answered and said to Esau, "Behold, I have made him lord over you, and all his brothers I have given to him for servants, and with grain and wine I have sustained him. What then can I do for you, my son?" ³⁸Esau said to his father, "Have you but one blessing, my father? Bless me, even me also, O my father." And Esau lifted up his voice and wept.

³⁹Then Isaac his father answered and said to him:

> "Behold, away from the fatness of the earth shall your dwelling be,
> and away from the dew of heaven on high.
> ⁴⁰By your sword you shall live,
> and you shall serve your brother;
> but when you grow restless
> you shall break his yoke from your neck."

⁴¹Now Esau hated Jacob because of the blessing with which his father had blessed him, and Esau said to himself, "The days of mourning for my father are approaching; then I will kill my brother Jacob." ⁴²But the words of Esau her older son were told to Rebekah. So she sent and called Jacob her younger son and said to him, "Behold, your brother Esau comforts himself about you by planning to kill you. ⁴³Now therefore, my son, obey my voice. Arise, flee to Laban my brother in Haran ⁴⁴and stay with him a while, until your brother's fury turns away—⁴⁵until your brother's anger turns away from you, and he forgets what you have done to him. Then I will send and bring you from there. Why should I be bereft of you both in one day?"

⁴⁶Then Rebekah said to Isaac, "I loathe my life because of the Hittite women. If Jacob marries one of the Hittite women like these, one of the women of the land, what good will my life be to me?"

Go Deeper

Esau was a careless man. He made a number of foolish mistakes in his life. We can certainly identify with him. He lost major opportunities and privileges because he was careless. We first see his careless attitude in an episode recorded in Genesis 25:29–34. It easily ranks as the dumbest mistake Esau ever made in his life. It's wise advice not to go grocery shopping when you're hungry. It's also wise not to negotiate birthrights when you're hungry.

According to this passage Jacob was home cooking stew while Esau was out in the woods. Jacob was experiencing the joy of cooking, and Esau, of course, was doing what he loved the most, as well. Esau arrived exhausted from hunting, but he failed to bring home game. He also

(continued)

Go Deeper Continued . . .

failed to see the connection between the *fun* he was having and the *food* he needed to have. The stew smelled so good that nothing else mattered at that moment. Where Esau failed to see danger, Jacob saw an opportunity.

In truth, both brothers made bad mistakes. Esau failed to take care of his daily needs or his birthright. Jacob failed to see anything wrong with taking advantage of his more vulnerable twin brother. Esau easily convinced himself he was starving. But he was not going to *die;* he was allowing a *physical* need to dictate his decisions. Meanwhile, Jacob was allowing an opportune moment to overrule his heart and conscience.

This can easily happen to us, too, if we fail to think eternally, biblically or wisely. Don't let the distractions of this world rob you of eternal perspective. You need to choose the wise road. Think about eternal values. Make smart decisions based on the Word of God.

I saac, the miracle child of Abraham and Sarah, didn't become a father until he was 60 years old. When Rebekah finally conceived, two things were apparent: first, her pregnancy was a divine gift; and second, her womb contained not one but two children. Rebekah was so uncomfortable that she wondered if something unusual was going on inside her. The Lord let her know that there was already animosity between her children that would be played out in generations to come.

Fast forward 70 years. Isaac was wisely preparing for the day of his death. In his preparation he asked his son Esau to make a special meal for him that would provide the occasion to pass on the patriarchal blessing. Isaac would actually live 43 more years, but he made important final preparations. It was an Eastern custom, a patriarchal tradition, to bless those whom one loved and cared for before one died. Jacob blessed all his children before he died. (See Gen. 48–49.) Deuteronomy 33:1 says, "This is the blessing with which Moses the man of God blessed the people of Israel before his death."

Eating and drinking were all part of this formal giving of the blessing. It's difficult to imagine that Isaac was ignorant of the divine purpose that God revealed to Rebekah while the twins struggled within her womb back in chapter 25. God had announced that Jacob

> *"God's Word makes it painfully clear that God's plan moved forward because it was His will, not because of the stellar character of the people involved."*

would get the blessing. But it was perhaps natural for him to love Esau as the firstborn. Meanwhile, Rebekah had her own reasons for having Jacob as her favorite. These parental choices created a rift in the family.

While Esau hunted for game to serve his father, Rebekah huddled with Jacob to devise plans to make sure he got the patriarchal blessing. Were Rebekah's motives pure or were they devious? Was she trying to put one over on Isaac here? That's what the text seems to imply. It looks like this is a classic case of the battle of the wills—Isaac versus Rebekah. Each one of them loved one son more than the other son, and each was willing to do whatever it took to see that son receive the covenant blessing.

How did Jacob play out in all this? Jacob was clearly more concerned about being caught than he was about doing the right thing. (See Gen. 27:11–12.) Jacob's only worry was his discovery, not his deceit. He had already displayed his talent for scheming when he tricked Esau into selling his birthright (25:29–34). Yet Jacob seemed unable at this point to see his own deceitful nature.

Rebekah understood that their actions could bring a curse on her and her son. She said, "Let your curse be on me, my son; only obey my voice, and go, bring them to me" (27:13). Mother and son were about to take advantage of their aging father and husband.

With the help of clothes, imitation hairy skin and roasted meat, Jacob did his best impression of his older brother. In order to deceive Isaac, Jacob had to lie repeatedly. Isaac sensed something wasn't quite right, but he couldn't see through Rebekah and Jacob's scheme. Isaac's hesitance was matched by Jacob's determination.

When Isaac questioned how "Esau" could be back with game so quickly, Jacob despicably attributed his speedy return to the blessing of God. Jacob's clever disguise even passed the touch test when Isaac felt his hair-covered arms: "So Jacob went near to Isaac his father, who felt him and said, 'The voice is Jacob's voice, but the hands are the hands of Esau'" (v. 22). The deception worked; Jacob got Isaac's blessing.

Even though the results occurred because of the sovereignty of God, the actors in this drama (Esau, Jacob, Isaac and Rebekah) didn't act in a way that pleased God. They got the right results in the wrong way. God's plan wasn't derailed, but the means used did not honor Him. Esau's carelessness and Jacob's scheming, combined with Isaac and Rebekah's favoritism, created a sinful environment. It preserved patterns in the family that carried into the next generations.

While Isaac seems to have been somewhat like his father, Abraham (see the almost identical problem with lying in Gen. 12:10–20 and Gen. 26:6–11), Jacob picked up his mother's traits. Jacob would later be on the receiving end of Rebekah's family's deceitful tendencies. Isaac seems to have been content to merely hold the Abrahamic blessing from God. It wasn't until he passed it on to Jacob that events began to unfold that revealed the scope of God's plan.

Abraham had a son, and Isaac had two sons. But Jacob fathered a nation. God's Word makes it painfully clear that God's plan moved forward because it was His will, not because of the stellar character of the people involved. God didn't reveal these flaws so we could look down on His people of the past, but so we could have hope that He can still work through people like us in the present.

Express It

Esau exemplifies careless living. Jacob approached life with cunning. This passage faithfully describes but doesn't prescribe the behavior of either brother. Talk to God about the degree to which you are allowing His values and Word to direct the decisions you make. Ask Him for wisdom to avoid both carelessness and cunning in your efforts to live for Him.

Consider It

As you read Genesis 25:19–27:46 consider these questions:

1) How were the twins born to Isaac and Rebekah different from each other?

2) Whose fault was the parental favoritism by Isaac and Rebekah? Why?

3) Why did Esau trade something of such great value for a bowl of stew?

4) What did Isaac do that revealed he didn't fully understand God's promise to him (see 26:1–11)?

5) Describe what this lesson's passage tells us about Jacob's character.

6) Why do you think Jacob went along with his mother's plan to deceive his father?

7) When have you noticed that God's will has been accomplished despite the efforts of people who have done everything wrong?

Lesson 11

On the Run

Rebekah was worried. Esau had threatened to kill Jacob as soon as Isaac died. How could she get Jacob out of harm's way? She resorted to her favorite tactic—trickery.

Read Genesis 28:1–31:55

Genesis 28, 31

Jacob Sent to Laban

28 Then Isaac called Jacob and blessed him and directed him, "You must not take a wife from the Canaanite women. ²Arise, go to Paddan-aram to the house of Bethuel your mother's father, and take as your wife from there one of the daughters of Laban your mother's brother. ³God Almighty bless you and make you fruitful and multiply you, that you may become a company of peoples. ⁴May he give the blessing of Abraham to you and to your offspring with you, that you may take possession of the land of your sojournings that God gave to Abraham!" ⁵Thus Isaac sent Jacob away. And he went to Paddan-aram, to Laban, the son of Bethuel the Aramean, the brother of Rebekah, Jacob's and Esau's mother.

Esau Marries an Ishmaelite

⁶Now Esau saw that Isaac had blessed Jacob and sent him away to Paddan-aram to take a wife from there, and that as he blessed him he directed him, "You must not take a wife from the Canaanite women," ⁷and that Jacob had obeyed his father and his mother and gone to Paddan-aram. ⁸So when Esau saw that the Canaanite women did not please Isaac his father, ⁹Esau went to Ishmael and took as his wife, besides the wives he had, Mahalath the daughter of Ishmael, Abraham's son, the sister of Nebaioth.

Jacob's Dream

¹⁰Jacob left Beersheba and went toward Haran. ¹¹And he came to a certain place and stayed there that night, because the sun had set. Taking one of the stones of the place, he put it under his head and lay down in that place to sleep. ¹²And he dreamed, and behold,

Key Verse

"Behold, I am with you and will keep you wherever you go, and will bring you back to this land. For I will not leave you until I have done what I have promised you" (Gen. 28:15).

there was a ladder set up on the earth, and the top of it reached to heaven. And behold, the angels of God were ascending and descending on it! ¹³And behold, the Lᴏʀᴅ stood above it and said, "I am the Lᴏʀᴅ, the God of Abraham your father and the God of Isaac. The land on which you lie I will give to you and to your offspring. ¹⁴Your offspring shall be like the dust of the earth, and you shall spread abroad to the west and to the east and to the north and to the south, and in you and your offspring shall all the families of the earth be blessed. ¹⁵Behold, I am with you and will keep you wherever you go, and will bring you back to this land. For I will not leave you until I have done what I have promised you." ¹⁶Then Jacob awoke from his sleep and said, "Surely the Lᴏʀᴅ is in this place, and I did not know it." ¹⁷And he was afraid and said, "How awesome is this place! This is none other than the house of God, and this is the gate of heaven."

¹⁸So early in the morning Jacob took the stone that he had put under his head and set it up for a pillar and poured oil on the top of it. ¹⁹He called the name of that place Bethel, but the name of the city was Luz at the first. ²⁰Then Jacob made a vow, saying, "If God will be with me and will keep me in this way that I go, and will give me bread to eat and

clothing to wear, ²¹so that I come again to my father's house in peace, then the Lord shall be my God, ²²and this stone, which I have set up for a pillar, shall be God's house. And of all that you give me I will give a full tenth to you."

* * * * * * * * * * * * * * *

Jacob Flees from Laban

31 Now Jacob heard that the sons of Laban were saying, "Jacob has taken all that was our father's, and from what was our father's he has gained all this wealth." ²And Jacob saw that Laban did not regard him with favor as before. ³Then the Lord said to Jacob, "Return to the land of your fathers and to your kindred, and I will be with you."

⁴So Jacob sent and called Rachel and Leah into the field where his flock was ⁵and said to them, "I see that your father does not regard me with favor as he did before. But the God of my father has been with me. ⁶You know that I have served your father with all my strength, ⁷yet your father has cheated me and changed my wages ten times. But God did not permit him to harm me. ⁸If he said, 'The spotted shall be your wages,' then all the flock bore spotted; and if he said, 'The striped shall be your wages,' then all the flock bore striped. ⁹Thus God has taken away the livestock of your father and given them to me. ¹⁰In the breeding season of the flock I lifted up my eyes and saw in a dream that the goats that mated with the flock were striped, spotted, and mottled. ¹¹Then the angel of God said to me in the dream, 'Jacob,' and I said, 'Here I am!' ¹²And he said, 'Lift up your eyes and see, all the goats that mate with the flock are striped, spotted, and mottled, for I have seen all that Laban is doing to you. ¹³I am the God of Bethel, where you anointed a pillar and made a vow to me. Now arise, go out from this land and return to the land of your kindred.'" ¹⁴Then Rachel and Leah answered and said to him, "Is there any portion or inheritance left to us in our father's house? ¹⁵Are we not regarded by him as foreigners? For he has sold us, and he has indeed devoured our money. ¹⁶All the wealth that God has taken away from our father belongs to us and to our children. Now then, whatever God has said to you, do."

¹⁷So Jacob arose and set his sons and his wives on camels. ¹⁸He drove away all his livestock, all his property that he had gained, the livestock in his possession that he had acquired in Paddan-aram, to go to the land of Canaan to his father Isaac. ¹⁹Laban had gone to shear his sheep, and Rachel stole her father's household gods. ²⁰And Jacob tricked Laban the Aramean, by not telling him that he intended to flee. ²¹He fled with all that he had and arose and crossed the Euphrates, and set his face toward the hill country of Gilead.

²²When it was told Laban on the third day that Jacob had fled, ²³he took his kinsmen with him and pursued him for seven days and followed close after him into the hill country of Gilead. ²⁴But God came to Laban the Aramean in a dream by night and said to him, "Be careful not to say anything to Jacob, either good or bad."

²⁵And Laban overtook Jacob. Now Jacob had pitched his tent in the hill country, and Laban with his kinsmen pitched tents in the hill country of Gilead. ²⁶And Laban said to Jacob, "What have you done, that you have tricked me and driven away my daughters like captives of the sword? ²⁷Why did you flee secretly and trick me, and did not tell me, so that I might have sent you away with mirth and songs, with tambourine and lyre? ²⁸And why did you not permit me to kiss my sons and my daughters farewell? Now you have done foolishly. ²⁹It is in my power to do you harm. But the God of your father spoke to me last night,

saying, 'Be careful not to say anything to Jacob, either good or bad.' ³⁰And now you have gone away because you longed greatly for your father's house, but why did you steal my gods?" ³¹Jacob answered and said to Laban, "Because I was afraid, for I thought that you would take your daughters from me by force. ³²Anyone with whom you find your gods shall not live. In the presence of our kinsmen point out what I have that is yours, and take it." Now Jacob did not know that Rachel had stolen them.

³³So Laban went into Jacob's tent and into Leah's tent and into the tent of the two female servants, but he did not find them. And he went out of Leah's tent and entered Rachel's. ³⁴Now Rachel had taken the household gods and put them in the camel's saddle and sat on them. Laban felt all about the tent, but did not find them. ³⁵And she said to her father, "Let not my lord be angry that I cannot rise before you, for the way of women is upon me." So he searched but did not find the household gods.

³⁶Then Jacob became angry and berated Laban. Jacob said to Laban, "What is my offense? What is my sin, that you have hotly pursued me? ³⁷For you have felt through all my goods; what have you found of all your household goods? Set it here before my kinsmen and your kinsmen, that they may decide between us two. ³⁸These twenty years I have been with you. Your ewes and your female goats have not miscarried, and I have not eaten the rams of your flocks. ³⁹What was torn by wild beasts I did not bring to you. I bore the loss of it myself. From my hand you required it, whether stolen by day or stolen by night. ⁴⁰There I was: by day the heat consumed me, and the cold by night, and my sleep fled from my eyes. ⁴¹These twenty years I have been in your house. I served you fourteen years for your two daughters, and six years for your flock, and you have changed my wages ten times. ⁴²If the God of my father, the God of Abraham and the Fear of Isaac, had not been on my side, surely now you would have sent me away empty-handed. God saw my affliction and the labor of my hands and rebuked you last night."

⁴³Then Laban answered and said to Jacob, "The daughters are my daughters, the children are my children, the flocks are my flocks, and all that you see is mine. But what can I do this day for these my daughters or for their children whom they have borne? ⁴⁴Come now, let us make a covenant, you and I. And let it be a witness between you and me." ⁴⁵So Jacob took a stone and set it up as a pillar. ⁴⁶And Jacob said to his kinsmen, "Gather stones." And they took stones and made a heap, and they ate there by the heap. ⁴⁷Laban called it Jegarsahadutha, but Jacob called it Galeed. ⁴⁸Laban said, "This heap is a witness between you and me today." Therefore he named it Galeed, ⁴⁹and Mizpah, for he said, "The Lᴏʀᴅ watch between you and me, when we are out of one another's sight. ⁵⁰If you oppress my daughters, or if you take wives besides my daughters, although no one is with us, see, God is witness between you and me."

⁵¹Then Laban said to Jacob, "See this heap and the pillar, which I have set between you and me. ⁵²This heap is a witness, and the pillar is a witness, that I will not pass over this heap to you, and you will not pass over this heap and this pillar to me, to do harm. ⁵³The God of Abraham and the God of Nahor, the God of their father, judge between us." So Jacob swore by the Fear of his father Isaac, ⁵⁴and Jacob offered a sacrifice in the hill country and called his kinsmen to eat bread. They ate bread and spent the night in the hill country.

⁵⁵Early in the morning Laban arose and kissed his grandchildren and his daughters and blessed them. Then Laban departed and returned home.

Go Deeper

Jacob's dream not only gave the young man a vivid encounter with the God of his fathers, but it also communicated powerful insights and promises about God's desired connection with people. If we have a connection with God, we have a connection with heaven. The key to the dream-ladder is that it goes all the way to heaven. It reaches from earth to heaven.

When we find God's ladder, we find God. There's only one ladder, one direct access to God. If you want to go to God's heaven, you have to go in God's way. Jesus said, "I am the way, and the truth, and the life. No one comes to the Father except through me" (John 14:6). Again, Jesus called Himself "the door" (John 10:7,9). When you discover Jesus Christ, when you put your faith in Him, it's the same as Jacob having this dream about a ladder that stretches all the way to God—except this isn't a dream. This is reality. Jesus is our Jacob's ladder. I hope you've trusted Him today.

Note seven promises/insights we can find in this revelation of God to Jacob:

1. God isn't an idea or force. God is separate and personal (Gen. 28:13).

2. Jacob's sleeping spot is the perpetual inheritance of his family, Israel (12:7–8; 28:13).

3. Jacob's descendants would multiply (28:14).

4. Jacob's descendants would be found throughout the earth (v. 14).

5. In Jacob's descendants, all other nations of the world would be blessed—the greatest example of this is Jesus (v. 14).

6. God promised to be with Jacob and bring him home (v. 15).

7. God promised never to leave Jacob's offspring but to accomplish His promises (v. 15).

J acob eventually had to leave home. Esau was still angry because Jacob and Rebekah had successfully obtained the blessing. His hatred was apparent enough that Rebekah had to come up with a plan to remove Jacob from the scene. The marriage prospects for the two boys gave her a perfect opportunity. One of the few things she and Isaac agreed about was their desire to see their sons married to people from their clan rather than the local Canaanites. Isaac agreed to let Jacob journey back to Haran in search of a wife.

Rebekah thought the tension would be relieved if Jacob would "arise, flee to Laban my brother in Haran and stay with him a while"

(Gen. 27:43–44). She really underestimated the time her dear son would be gone (playing favorites in the family meant 20 years of pain for everybody).

For Jacob, the time away from home began and ended with unforgettable encounters with God (28:10–17; 32:22–32). It also involved three major episodes where Jacob was on the run. First, he ran from his brother's anger. Then he ran from Laban's control. And all along he was running from God.

Several days into his journey, God met Jacob in a dream at Bethel, a location that became a significant place for worship in Israel's history: "And he dreamed, and behold, there was a ladder set up on the earth, and the top of it reached to heaven. And behold, the angels of God were ascending and descending on it! And behold, the Lord stood above it and said, 'I am the Lord, the God of Abraham your father and the God of Isaac. The land on which you lie I will give to you and to your offspring'" (28:12–13). Despite Jacob's history of deceitfulness, God confirmed the blessing on him. Jacob, for his part, responded with a carefully worded promise to treat God as God.

Although one of his reasons for leaving home was to find a wife, Jacob probably didn't expect to run into her his first day in Haran. But Jacob and Rachel are one of the "love-at-first-sight" stories we find in the Bible. In a striking reversal of history, the son of a woman who once eagerly served water to the camel train of Abraham's servant now served water to the sheep of his mother's brother's own lovely daughter.

It didn't take long for Laban to notice that Jacob was smitten. Though Jacob was old enough to marry and certainly a good match for his daughter, Laban also knew that he had little of his wealth or inheritance with him. But Laban was ready to negotiate with this young man who seemed to have God's favor. When Jacob suggested a seven-year labor contract in exchange for the hand of Rachel, Laban agreed. But he had a lot more in mind. Eventually he manipulated Jacob into 20 years of indentured service.

Seven years after arriving in Laban's house, Jacob received two wives and a contract for seven more years of service. Though Rachel was the love of his life, her sister Leah began bearing sons for Jacob—

> *"For Jacob, the time away from home began and ended with unforgettable encounters with God. . . . Despite Jacob's history of deceitfulness, God confirmed the blessing on him."*

four within a few years—while Rachel remained barren. This caused a great deal of strife in Jacob's tents. By the time Jacob left Laban, he had 11 sons by four different women.

As the second seven-year stretch came to a close, Laban still had plans to keep Jacob around. He realized he had prospered greatly with Jacob as his herdsman. So, he tried to bargain more years of work from Jacob, who by this time was on to his father-in-law. The younger schemer outwitted the older. Clever breeding practices soon had Jacob's flocks flourishing while Laban's languished. Jacob was now following the "letter" of their business arrangement but was getting most of the real benefits. Laban's sons were suspicious. Tensions mounted. Jacob sensed God was telling him it was time to go home (31:3).

Jacob also sensed Laban would do everything in his power to prevent Jacob's departure. So, with his wives' approval, they all simply packed and left while Laban went to shear his sheep. When Laban discovered Jacob was gone, he went in hot pursuit. We don't know what would have happened, but God intervened and warned Laban to treat Jacob respectfully (v. 24). Their encounter on the road was tense. Laban made the most of his one "just cause"—his house idols were missing. Rachel never revealed why she stole the idols. We can guess the theft was a gesture of anger and resentment against her father.

In the end, Laban and Jacob separated with a covenant pledge: "The LORD watch between you and me, when we are out of one another's sight" (v. 49). While this covenant is often called "the Mizpah benediction," it is more of a formal agreement of non-aggression. This closed a significant chapter in Jacob's life and shifted his full attention on what might be waiting for him at home.

Express It

Jacob's journey illustrates the combination of human decisions, God's guidance and God's sovereign will. Our choices matter, but they don't derail God's plans. As you pray today, focus on your confidence that God will provide you with journey wisdom and bring you to the places where He wants you to serve Him.

Consider It

As you read Genesis 28:1–31:55, consider these questions:

1) What was the situation at home when Jacob left?

2) Why did Esau marry local women?

3) What do you notice as significant in Jacob's dream?

4) What excuse did Laban give for substituting Leah for Rachel on the wedding night?

5) When do you think Jacob realized Laban was manipulating him?

6) How do Jacob's marriages illustrate the problems of polygamy?

7) What led to Jacob's departure from Laban's house?

A Fearful Homecoming

Unresolved conflicts tend to create fear. The longer we put off settling a difference, the more likely we are to fear the outcome. Jacob and Esau had a long-standing conflict that had to be resolved, and Jacob wasn't sure how things would turn out.

Read Genesis 32:1–36:43

Genesis 32

Jacob Fears Esau

32 Jacob went on his way, and the angels of God met him. ²And when Jacob saw them he said, "This is God's camp!" So he called the name of that place Mahanaim.

³And Jacob sent messengers before him to Esau his brother in the land of Seir, the country of Edom, ⁴instructing them, "Thus you shall say to my lord Esau: Thus says your servant Jacob, 'I have sojourned with Laban and stayed until now. ⁵I have oxen, donkeys, flocks, male servants, and female servants. I have sent to tell my lord, in order that I may find favor in your sight.'"

⁶And the messengers returned to Jacob, saying, "We came to your brother Esau, and he is coming to meet you, and there are four hundred men with him." ⁷Then Jacob was greatly afraid and distressed. He divided the people who were with him, and the flocks and herds and camels, into two camps, ⁸thinking, "If Esau comes to the one camp and attacks it, then the camp that is left will escape."

⁹And Jacob said, "O God of my father Abraham and God of my father Isaac, O LORD who said to me, 'Return to your country and to your kindred, that I may do you good,' ¹⁰I am not worthy of the least of all the deeds of steadfast love and all the faithfulness that you have shown to your servant, for with only my staff I crossed this Jordan, and now I have become two camps. ¹¹Please deliver me from the hand of my brother, from the hand of Esau, for I fear him, that he may come and attack me, the mothers with the children. ¹²But you said, 'I will surely do you good, and make your offspring as the sand of the sea, which cannot be numbered for multitude.'"

¹³So he stayed there that night, and from what he had with him he took

Key Verse

Then he said, "Your name shall no longer be called Jacob, but Israel, for you have striven with God and with men, and have prevailed" (Gen. 32:28).

a present for his brother Esau, ¹⁴two hundred female goats and twenty male goats, two hundred ewes and twenty rams, ¹⁵thirty milking camels and their calves, forty cows and ten bulls, twenty female donkeys and ten male donkeys. ¹⁶These he handed over to his servants, every drove by itself, and said to his servants, "Pass on ahead of me and put a space between drove and drove." ¹⁷He instructed the first, "When Esau my brother meets you and asks you, 'To whom do you belong? Where are you going? And whose are these ahead of you?' ¹⁸then you shall say, 'They belong to your servant Jacob. They are a present sent to my lord Esau. And moreover, he is behind us.'" ¹⁹He likewise instructed the second and the third and all who followed the droves, "You shall say the same thing to Esau when you find him, ²⁰and you shall say, 'Moreover, your servant Jacob is behind us.'" For he thought, "I may appease him with the present that goes ahead of me, and afterward I shall see his face. Perhaps he will accept me." ²¹So the present passed on ahead of him, and he himself stayed that night in the camp.

Jacob Wrestles with God

²²The same night he arose and took his two wives, his two female servants, and his eleven children, and crossed the ford of the Jabbok. ²³He took them and sent

them across the stream, and everything else that he had. ²⁴And Jacob was left alone. And a man wrestled with him until the breaking of the day. ²⁵When the man saw that he did not prevail against Jacob, he touched his hip socket, and Jacob's hip was put out of joint as he wrestled with him. ²⁶Then he said, "Let me go, for the day has broken." But Jacob said, "I will not let you go unless you bless me." ²⁷And he said to him, "What is your name?" And he said, "Jacob." ²⁸Then he said, "Your name shall no longer be called Jacob, but Israel, for you have striven with God and with men, and have prevailed." ²⁹Then Jacob asked him, "Please tell me your name." But he said, "Why is it that you ask my name?" And there he blessed him. ³⁰So Jacob called the name of the place Peniel, saying, "For I have seen God face to face, and yet my life has been delivered." ³¹The sun rose upon him as he passed Penuel, limping because of his hip. ³²Therefore to this day the people of Israel do not eat the sinew of the thigh that is on the hip socket, because he touched the socket of Jacob's hip on the sinew of the thigh.

Go Deeper

Jacob's story allows us to think about "wrestling" with God. How do we fight God and win? Let me suggest several ways we can prepare to wrestle with God successfully.

First of all, like Jacob, we have to be pliable in God's hands. We have to allow God to do with us what God chooses to do with us. If we are not flexible in the hands of God, we will be broken in a fight with God. We must not be rigid in our plans or choices, knowing God can overrule.

Secondly, if we want to win in a fight with God, we must be willing to admit that we're not worthy of any of God's blessings (Gen. 32:10). We don't enter a fight with God thinking we are worthy of winning. All we think about is that we're worthy of losing. We can't appreciate God's blessings until we realize we don't deserve any of them.

Thirdly, if we want to win a fight with God, we must always trust the promises of God. Jacob did that. He recounted some of those promises when he cried out to God (32:9–12). When we're facing a fight with God and we don't know how it's going to turn out, we must remember He loves us. We can trust the promises of God even when we are in the fight of our lives with Him.

Fourth, we must be ready to engage and interact with God. We must willingly enter the fray with God and tell Him how we feel, what we're thinking and even what we want. We need to spend enough time in His Word to let Him tell us what He's thinking.

Fifth, if we want to win a fight with God, we must be ready to accept the consequences of our fight. Jacob prevailed, but Jacob was lame the rest of his life. It's not a lack of reverence on our part to engage in dialogue with God as long as we do so submissively and with the right heart attitude.

J acob came home afraid. His ally, his mother, was no longer alive. Sometime during the 20 years he was with Laban, Rebekah died. After Jacob's departure, Rebekah isn't mentioned again in Genesis except for the note in 49:31 that she was buried with Isaac in the family plot. For all he knew, Esau was still angry over the birthright and blessing Jacob had stolen. Jacob by nature was a "runner" not a fighter. Even God's assurance didn't remove Jacob's dread over meeting his brother.

His concerns seemed to be justified when the men he sent to Esau to announce his arrival returned with news that Esau was coming to meet him with 400 men. Jacob's survival instincts kicked in. He not only divided his camp in hopes of ensuring that at least one group would survive an attack, but he also prepared an astonishing gift for his brother (32:14–15). Then he crossed the Jabbok stream with his immediate family and put his fate in God's hands.

Later that night, Jacob was alone with God. Genesis 32:24 says, "And Jacob was left alone. And a man wrestled with him until the breaking of the day." Not a bad place to be—alone with God. Was this a real fight, or did Jacob just have another dream here? We don't see anything in the narrative that mentions sleep or a dream or a vision, so I have to conclude it was a real conflict. Other Scripture affirms this conclusion and identifies the "man" as an angel. (See Hos. 12:3–6.)

So, what's the purpose of this all-night fight? The purpose was to revive Jacob's discouraged and despondent spirit. The purpose was to convince him it was okay to meet Esau. The purpose was to convince him that he could face all future challenges with confidence in God. God knew His purposes would not be accomplished unless they were driven into Jacob with a fight.

The wrestling match was designed specifically not to discourage Jacob but to encourage him. How do we know that? Genesis 32:25 says, "When the man saw that he did not prevail against Jacob, he touched his hip socket, and Jacob's hip was put out of joint as he wrestled with him." We must never forget that we only win the battles with God that God wants us to win. If you're involved in your own wrestling match with God, remember that any victory God gives you and anything you learn from this battle is God's gift to you.

"*Even the injuries God may bring into our lives eventually prove to be for our benefit.*"

Could this angel have beaten Jacob? Certainly! But God purposefully did not prevail in this battle. God touched Jacob's hip, and He put it out of joint. Now, there was nothing Jacob could do here. The angel had performed hip-displacement, and there was no hip-replacement surgery in those days. Jacob would forever walk with a limp, which would forever remind him of the day he fought it out with God.

Sometimes when we fight it out with God, God allows us to have some victory. God allows us to prevail but not without a cost. Jacob is crippled in this wrestling match, and he's going to walk with a limp the rest of his days.

Meanwhile, the wrestling match became a draw. Jacob grew bold now because he realized there was no clear-cut winner. So, when the angel said, "Let me go for the day has broken" (v. 26), Jacob said, "I will not let you go unless you bless me" (v. 26). Jacob already had his father's blessing, the one he cheated from his twin brother. Now he wanted a legitimate blessing that would be won by combat, not stolen by deception, and God gave it to him.

God's blessing on Jacob was a new name. In Genesis 32:28 the angel said, "Your name shall no longer be called Jacob, but Israel, for you have striven with God and with men, and have prevailed." The angel changed Jacob's name to Israel, which means "prince with God." How would you like to have your name changed from something derogatory like "supplanter" to something positive like "prince with God"? Jacob walked away from his encounter with God with a new name and a limp.

When you and I fight it out with God, we're amazed too. We're amazed that we survive that fight. We're amazed that God doesn't kill us; we're amazed that God doesn't take His blessing from us. The more I get to know God, the more amazed I become at His character. Not only is God willing to engage us in life's struggles, but He's also willing to bless us through them. We may be hurt, but we will also be changed. Even the injuries God may bring into our lives eventually prove to be for our benefit.

When all is said and done, we have to make sure that our lives are different after we fight it out with God. If they aren't, it really wasn't worth the fight, was it? It's possible, like Jacob, for you and me to wrestle with God and come out alive and, in fact, come out blessed, but also to come out lame. We have to make sure when we engage in the battle, after our fight with God, we are more like God and not bitter at Him.

Express It

Jacob's limp became a constant reminder of God's blessing. Are there difficult memories, wounds and limitations that serve this kind of positive effect in your life? Consider this question as you pray today; and if God helps you identify some of these, give Him thanks.

Consider It

As you read Genesis 32:1–36:43, consider these questions:

1) How did Jacob deal with fear? What were some parts of his strategy?

2) How do you deal with fear?

3) What point did God make by leaving Jacob with a limp?

4) Given his elevated fear, what might Jacob have learned from his actual encounter with Esau?

5) What lessons do you find in the episode involving Dinah, Shechem and Jacob's sons (Gen. 34)?

6) How did God continue to shape Jacob's life in Genesis 35?

7) Compare Genesis 35:19–20 and 49:31–32. What significance do you see in the different burial sites for Rachel and Leah?

Lesson
13

Joseph, the Dreamer

Christ's followers sometimes encounter ridicule and conflict in this world. Following God's plan for our lives, living by His guidelines and surrendering to Him, is in direct opposition to the world. That didn't matter to Joseph. He lived a life of integrity, determined to please God—whatever the consequences.

Read Genesis 37:1–39:23

Genesis 37

Joseph's Dreams

37 Jacob lived in the land of his father's sojournings, in the land of Canaan.

²These are the generations of Jacob.

Joseph, being seventeen years old, was pasturing the flock with his brothers. He was a boy with the sons of Bilhah and Zilpah, his father's wives. And Joseph brought a bad report of them to their father. ³Now Israel loved Joseph more than any other of his sons, because he was the son of his old age. And he made him a robe of many colors. ⁴But when his brothers saw that their father loved him more than all his brothers, they hated him and could not speak peacefully to him.

⁵Now Joseph had a dream, and when he told it to his brothers they hated him even more. ⁶He said to them, "Hear this dream that I have dreamed: ⁷Behold, we were binding sheaves in the field, and behold, my sheaf arose and stood upright. And behold, your sheaves gathered around it and bowed down to my sheaf." ⁸His brothers said to him, "Are you indeed to reign over us? Or are you indeed to rule over us?" So they hated him even more for his dreams and for his words.

⁹Then he dreamed another dream and told it to his brothers and said, "Behold, I have dreamed another dream. Behold, the sun, the moon, and eleven stars were bowing down to me." ¹⁰But when he told it to his father and to his brothers, his father rebuked him and said to him, "What is this dream that you have dreamed? Shall I and your mother and your brothers indeed come to bow ourselves to the ground before you?" ¹¹And his brothers were jealous of him, but his father kept the saying in mind.

Key Verse

But the LORD was with Joseph and showed him steadfast love and gave him favor in the sight of the keeper of the prison (Gen. 39:21).

Joseph Sold by His Brothers

¹²Now his brothers went to pasture their father's flock near Shechem. ¹³And Israel said to Joseph, "Are not your brothers pasturing the flock at Shechem? Come, I will send you to them." And he said to him, "Here I am." ¹⁴So he said to him, "Go now, see if it is well with your brothers and with the flock, and bring me word." So he sent him from the Valley of Hebron, and he came to Shechem. ¹⁵And a man found him wandering in the fields. And the man asked him, "What are you seeking?" ¹⁶"I am seeking my brothers," he said. "Tell me, please, where they are pasturing the flock." ¹⁷And the man said, "They have gone away, for I heard them say, 'Let us go to Dothan.'" So Joseph went after his brothers and found them at Dothan.

¹⁸They saw him from afar, and before he came near to them they conspired against him to kill him. ¹⁹They said to one another, "Here comes this dreamer. ²⁰Come now, let us kill him and throw him into one of the pits. Then we will say that a fierce animal has devoured him, and we will see what will become of his dreams." ²¹But when Reuben heard it, he rescued him out of their hands, saying, "Let us not take his life." ²²And Reuben said to them, "Shed no blood; throw him into this pit here in the wilderness, but

do not lay a hand on him"—that he might rescue him out of their hand to restore him to his father. ²³So when Joseph came to his brothers, they stripped him of his robe, the robe of many colors that he wore. ²⁴And they took him and threw him into a pit. The pit was empty; there was no water in it.

²⁵Then they sat down to eat. And looking up they saw a caravan of Ishmaelites coming from Gilead, with their camels bearing gum, balm, and myrrh, on their way to carry it down to Egypt. ²⁶Then Judah said to his brothers, "What profit is it if we kill our brother and conceal his blood? ²⁷Come, let us sell him to the Ishmaelites, and let not our hand be upon him, for he is our brother, our own flesh." And his brothers listened to him. ²⁸Then Midianite traders passed by. And they drew Joseph up and lifted him out of the pit, and sold him to the Ishmaelites for twenty shekels of silver. They took Joseph to Egypt.

²⁹When Reuben returned to the pit and saw that Joseph was not in the pit, he tore his clothes ³⁰and returned to his brothers and said, "The boy is gone, and I, where shall I go?" ³¹Then they took Joseph's robe and slaughtered a goat and dipped the robe in the blood. ³²And they sent the robe of many colors and brought it to their father and said, "This we have found; please identify whether it is your son's robe or not." ³³And he identified it and said, "It is my son's robe. A fierce animal has devoured him. Joseph is without doubt torn to pieces." ³⁴Then Jacob tore his garments and put sackcloth on his loins and mourned for his son many days. ³⁵All his sons and all his daughters rose up to comfort him, but he refused to be comforted and said, "No, I shall go down to Sheol to my son, mourning." Thus his father wept for him. ³⁶Meanwhile the Midianites had sold him in Egypt to Potiphar, an officer of Pharaoh, the captain of the guard.

Go Deeper

It was his father's heart and compassion for his children that caused Jacob to send his son Joseph to find his brothers. That's exactly the way it is with God. It is His heart of compassion for us that caused Him to send His Son from heaven to find us. But Jesus did more than Joseph did. Joseph only sought his brothers. Luke 19:10 says that Jesus came to seek and to save those who were lost. Joseph could locate his brothers, but he couldn't help them. Jesus could both locate us and bring salvation to us.

When Joseph showed up, his brothers wanted to kill him. How true of people. They want to kill the person who can save them. The mob wanted to kill Jesus, the only person who could save them.

Notice the parallels between Joseph and Jesus. Joseph never did anything that was a detriment to his character. He told his father about his brothers' sins. That was an indication of his concern for the holiness of his father.

Joseph told the truth, even when the truth was unacceptable to those around

(continued)

Go Deeper Continued . . .

him. He didn't give up his godliness even when it irritated his brothers. He had to learn hard lessons through suffering, but he didn't have to learn to tell the truth.

Joseph didn't deserve the hatred and the envy of his brothers. But, though despised, he didn't respond aggressively toward his brothers. How much like Jesus he is. And how much like Jesus you and I need to be when what we do irritates those around us because of their sin.

Joseph faithfully executed the will of his father—even though it would have been much more comfortable for him, much safer for him, to stay in Hebron. Comfort was not the issue. He kept searching until he found them, even though they responded with cruelty, mockery and the betrayal of selling him into slavery.

And, finally, Joseph didn't respond negatively to his brothers' ridicule. In fact, he didn't respond at all. Joseph trusted God. Even when everything turned into chaos, he continued to trust.

Be like Joseph because Joseph was like Jesus. Don't go out of your way to irritate people but do the right thing regardless—because doing the right thing is doing the will of the Father, and only the will of the Father prospers us.

The Book of Genesis is full of memorable people—like Adam and Eve, Noah, Abraham, Isaac, and Jacob. But in Genesis 37, the story shifts to Jacob's son Joseph, a good and righteous man, a man whose character and integrity are about as strong as anyone we find in the Old Testament. That doesn't mean that Joseph didn't have his problems. He learned his share of hard lessons. But he had a heart for God. And as we all discover sooner or later, sometimes problems arise *because* we try to live a life that pleases God.

Living to please God always involves choices that go against the flow of the world. Following God's leading creates problems because we are moving against the current. The world is going one way; we're going the other. That was part of Joseph's problem. He wasn't always popular, but he was doing what was right. His brothers had a different agenda, and that created conflict. The vengeful actions of the brothers can be explained by a number of developments.

First, Joseph brought back a negative report to Jacob about the behavior of some of his brothers (Gen. 37:1–2). We're not told what

"*Following God's leading creates problems because we are moving against the current. The world is going one way; we're going the other.*"

he said, but apparently his brothers were sinning in some way and Joseph's character wouldn't allow him to look the other way and allow his half-brothers to continue their sin. So, he reported it to his father. That irritated his siblings.

Second, Jacob showed favoritism toward Joseph (37:3–4). Despite the painful lessons from his own past, Jacob repeated his parents' mistakes: "Now Israel loved Joseph more than any other of his sons, because he was the son of his old age. And he made him a robe of many colors" (v. 3). Jacob compounded the problem by making his preferential treatment obvious. The robe indicated a different "pecking order" among the brothers, and they wouldn't have it.

Third, Joseph threw dry kindling on the embers of their hatred by describing his dream about the sheaves of grain. Here Joseph's forthrightness got him in trouble. He may not have meant to brag, but that's how his brothers took it (vv. 5–11). The interpretation of his dreams wasn't that difficult, but his brothers were offended by the idea that they would ever bow down to Joseph.

Fourth, Joseph's second dream confirmed the theme of the first and stoked the anger of his brothers. Even his father took offense over the second dream, in which his parents would bow.

Please notice that everything that Joseph did, he did with the proper motivation. He didn't do anything that God hadn't put in his mind. The brothers thought that Joseph was about to be elevated to the chief of the sons of the family—but God had a lot more in mind than Joseph's being chief of the family. God was going to elevate Joseph, but not in any way these brothers could have ever guessed.

When anger is present, can envy be far behind? The brothers got angry, became envious and then took action. Jacob unwittingly provided the perfect opportunity for his irritated siblings to act against Joseph (vv. 12–36).

Jacob sent his son, the dreamer, on an errand to check on his brothers' welfare. Jacob's favorite may have been Joseph, but he cared for his other sons. It took some effort, but Joseph found his brothers (traveling about 70 miles). They could hardly believe he had been "delivered" to them. They almost immediately decided to kill their dreamer brother. Only Reuben had pangs of conscience and spared his life. Then another apparent coincidence developed in the form of a caravan of Ishmaelite traders. The brothers came up with a new plan—to sell their brother as a slave. They would transform his dreams into nightmares. Joseph would later inform them what was really happening: "You meant evil against me, but God meant it for good" (50:20).

This episode in Joseph's life ends with his brothers convincing their father of his death at the claws and fangs of a wild animal. At the same time Joseph was being sold to a man named Potiphar in Egypt. The next years would test Joseph's dreams and his character. (See Gen. 39–40.) He displayed remarkable resilience. The same God who gave Joseph his dreams made sure they came true. As this lesson's key verse reminds us, the "Lord was with him" (39:21).

Express It

Joseph's dreams were about God's purpose in his life. Three times in this lesson's passage we read that "the Lord was with" Joseph (39:2, 21, 23). In what ways does your awareness that God is with you affect the way you live? Talk to God about His purposes for your life. Tell Him your dreams, and ask Him to show you which ones are from Him.

Consider It

As you read Genesis 37:1–39:23, consider these questions:

1) We know how Jacob's sons felt toward Joseph, but how do you think they felt toward their father?

_____

_____

2) The story picks up with Joseph probably about 17 years old. What experiences do you think shaped him the most to that point?

_____

_____

3) Why did God give Joseph his dreams?

_____

_____

4) What kept the brothers from killing Joseph?

_____

_____

5) How did Jacob deal with the news that his favorite son, Joseph, was apparently dead?

_____

_____

6) What lessons do you find in the episode between Judah and Tamar?

_____

_____

7) What do you think was the most difficult part of Joseph's life in Potiphar's house? Why?

_____

_____

8) How do we know Joseph's dreams were still alive when he was falsely thrown into prison?

_____

_____

Joseph, the Leader

Too many people base their lives on "if and when."
They spend their lives thinking, "If I win the lottery or
my ship comes in . . ." Others say, "When this is done,
then I'll do what's important, meaningful, necessary."
Joseph never related to that mentality. He lived in the
here and now.

Read Genesis 40:1–45:28

Genesis 40:1–41:14

Joseph Interprets Two Prisoners' Dreams

40 Some time after this, the cupbearer of the king of Egypt and his baker committed an offense against their lord the king of Egypt. ²And Pharaoh was angry with his two officers, the chief cupbearer and the chief baker, ³and he put them in custody in the house of the captain of the guard, in the prison where Joseph was confined. ⁴The captain of the guard appointed Joseph to be with them, and he attended them. They continued for some time in custody.

⁵And one night they both dreamed— the cupbearer and the baker of the king of Egypt, who were confined in the prison—each his own dream, and each dream with its own interpretation. ⁶When Joseph came to them in the morning, he saw that they were troubled. ⁷So he asked Pharaoh's officers who were with him in custody in his master's house, "Why are your faces downcast today?" ⁸They said to him, "We have had dreams, and there is no one to interpret them." And Joseph said to them, "Do not interpretations belong to God? Please tell them to me."

⁹So the chief cupbearer told his dream to Joseph and said to him, "In my dream there was a vine before me, ¹⁰and on the vine there were three branches. As soon as it budded, its blossoms shot forth, and the clusters ripened into grapes. ¹¹Pharaoh's cup was in my hand, and I took the grapes and pressed them into Pharaoh's cup and placed the cup in Pharaoh's hand." ¹²Then Joseph said to him, "This is its interpretation: the three branches are three days. ¹³In three days Pharaoh will lift up your head and restore you to your office, and you shall place Pharaoh's cup in his hand as formerly, when you were his cupbearer. ¹⁴Only remember me, when it is well with you, and please do me the kindness to

Key Verse

Then Pharaoh said to Joseph, "Since God has shown you all this, there is none so discerning and wise as you are" (Gen. 41:39).

mention me to Pharaoh, and so get me out of this house. ¹⁵For I was indeed stolen out of the land of the Hebrews, and here also I have done nothing that they should put me into the pit."

¹⁶When the chief baker saw that the interpretation was favorable, he said to Joseph, "I also had a dream: there were three cake baskets on my head, ¹⁷and in the uppermost basket there were all sorts of baked food for Pharaoh, but the birds were eating it out of the basket on my head." ¹⁸And Joseph answered and said, "This is its interpretation: the three baskets are three days. ¹⁹In three days Pharaoh will lift up your head—from you!—and hang you on a tree. And the birds will eat the flesh from you."

²⁰On the third day, which was Pharaoh's birthday, he made a feast for all his servants and lifted up the head of the chief cupbearer and the head of the chief baker among his servants. ²¹He restored the chief cupbearer to his position, and he placed the cup in Pharaoh's hand. ²²But he hanged the chief baker, as Joseph had interpreted to them. ²³Yet the chief cupbearer did not remember Joseph, but forgot him.

Joseph Interprets Pharaoh's Dreams

41 After two whole years, Pharaoh dreamed that he was standing by the Nile, ²and behold, there came up out of the Nile seven cows attractive and plump, and they fed in the reed grass. ³And behold, seven other cows, ugly and thin, came up out of the Nile after them, and stood by the other cows on the bank of the Nile. ⁴And the ugly, thin cows ate up the seven attractive, plump cows. And Pharaoh awoke. ⁵And he fell asleep and dreamed a second time. And behold, seven ears of grain, plump and good, were growing on one stalk. ⁶And behold, after them sprouted seven ears, thin and blighted by the east wind. ⁷And the thin ears swallowed up the seven plump, full ears. And Pharaoh awoke, and behold, it was a dream. ⁸So in the morning his spirit was troubled, and he sent and called for all the magicians of Egypt and all its wise men. Pharaoh told them his dreams, but there was none who could interpret them to Pharaoh.

⁹Then the chief cupbearer said to Pharaoh, "I remember my offenses today. ¹⁰When Pharaoh was angry with his servants and put me and the chief baker in custody in the house of the captain of the guard, ¹¹we dreamed on the same night, he and I, each having a dream with its own interpretation. ¹²A young Hebrew was there with us, a servant of the captain of the guard. When we told him, he interpreted our dreams to us, giving an interpretation to each man according to his dream. ¹³And as he interpreted to us, so it came about. I was restored to my office, and the baker was hanged."

¹⁴Then Pharaoh sent and called Joseph, and they quickly brought him out of the pit. And when he had shaved himself and changed his clothes, he came in before Pharaoh.

Go Deeper

Joseph's brothers made two trips to Egypt to buy grain. They repeatedly bowed before Joseph, fulfilling his dream. But Joseph, not interested in revenge but in reconciliation, devised a plan that would lead to confession and repentance on their part. He went to great and generous lengths to teach them a profound lesson.

In Genesis 44:15 Joseph confronted his brothers. The turning point in the story is at 44:16–17: "And Judah said, 'What shall we say to my lord? What shall we speak? Or how can we clear ourselves? God has found out the guilt of your servants; behold, we are my lord's servants, both we and he also in whose

hand the cup has been found.' But he said, 'Far be it from me that I should do so! Only the man in whose hand the cup was found shall be my servant. But as for you, go up in peace to your father.'"

Joseph's last statement was really bad news for his brothers. Joseph was about to keep Benjamin and send the rest of them home to their father. The others knew that could never happen. It would kill Jacob. The brothers had reached the end of the line.

In Genesis 44:18–34, Judah "spilled the beans." The situation allowed the brothers to experience firsthand what they had done to Joseph. Instead of taking revenge, he created an

(continued)

Go Deeper Continued . . .

opportunity for reconciliation. Joseph's behavior must be viewed as a well-thought-out plan to bring the brothers to repentance. You can read about that kind of plan in Hebrews 12:7–11.

Clearly Joseph's purposes in the test he made for the brothers were then realized. They had grown tender toward their aging father, and true brotherly affection was now shown toward each other and especially toward Benjamin. The brothers finally came to grips with their sin. It's a great picture of what you and I need to do, too, if we want to be right with God and spend eternity with Him.

Does God have a sense of humor? He certainly has a sense of timing. And timing, they say, is at the heart of humor. The very things Joseph could have deeply resented as the cause of his troubles in life—his dreams and the dreams of others—turned out to be the amazing key that revealed God's plan for Joseph.

Joseph had two vivid dreams when he was 17 (Gen. 37). They indicated that he would have a place of honor even his family would recognize. For more than a decade almost every new circumstance Joseph faced seemed to mock the meaning of those dreams. His brothers resented and rejected him, selling him into slavery. He was resold in Egypt to Potiphar. But though he served his master faithfully and brought blessings to Potiphar's house, he was also subjected to sexual harassment by Potiphar's wife. When he wouldn't yield to her seductions, she betrayed him. He ended up in prison. By human standards, he was getting progressively further from a place of honor. From favorite son, he had been demoted to slave. Now, the slave was a prisoner with no hope of parole.

There, Joseph faced two new dreams—the dreams of the baker and the cupbearer. Given his history, Joseph might have been tempted to stay as far away as possible from his or anyone else's dreams. His dreams certainly hadn't come true and didn't show any signs of ever being fulfilled. Yet, right here in the account we have one of the most perceptive statements of faith found in Scripture:

" The very things Joseph could have deeply resented as the cause of his troubles in life—his dreams and the dreams of others—turned out to be the amazing key that revealed God's plan for Joseph. "

"And Joseph said to them, 'Do not interpretations belong to God? Please tell them to me'" (40:8).

If interpretations belong to God, so do fulfillments. Joseph was still faithfully waiting. Joseph had no way of knowing that helping these two men would eventually take him to the second highest place in the kingdom of Egypt. He was simply responding with integrity in the situation that faced him. He would wait two more years because the cupbearer who had been restored to his position in the palace forgot Joseph in the prison. What we know from Joseph's actions and responses was that he wasn't living for "if" and "when." His life and future were in God's hands, and his primary responsibility was to pay attention to the choices and decisions that were before him now.

We don't know if Joseph ever chuckled over the fact that dreams showed up in his life in pairs. The Pharaoh eventually had a set of dreams that rocked the realm. Both dreams were vivid and troubling. They presented pleasant circumstances followed by disturbing images. None of Pharaoh's "magicians and wise men" could interpret the dreams, but they seemed ominous. That jogged the cupbearer's memory. He finally told Pharaoh about his own experience with dreams and Joseph's exact interpretation. The king immediately ordered Joseph hauled from the prison and brought to the palace.

Joseph must have been quite a sight, for despite the urgency of the king's orders, he took time to clean up (41:14). We aren't told what he was thinking, but his pattern suggests that he was calm and confident that this was another step in God's unfolding plan. He took no credit for the interpretation of dreams, but told Pharaoh the same thing he had told the cupbearer and baker—such things were in God's hands. It is almost impossible for us to imagine sleeping one night in a prison and the next in a royal suite. But that word *impossible* characterizes most of the things that God does. Jesus put it best: "What is impossible with men is possible with God" (Luke 18:27).

Because Joseph operated continuously in the present, he was able to visualize and verbalize a wise plan of action, even as he described for Pharaoh the significance of his dreams. He knew these dreams were an opportunity from God to prepare for something bad by making wise use of the intervening good.

As we read Joseph's report to Pharaoh, we can't help but think that Joseph was unaware he was applying for a job. He was merely giving his assessment of the necessary actions to be taken— something he had probably done for both Potiphar and for the jailer. Even Pharaoh could see that a man of such vision and connection with God was the most logical choice to supervise the plan. Elevating Joseph to second-in-command was a no-brainer for Pharaoh. The stakes were clear: if the promised prosperity didn't occur, then Joseph was in trouble. But if God proved faithful, Egypt would be rescued from disaster. God was simply putting the surprising, delightful and unexpected finishing touches on this chapter of His great plan. Joseph's dreams would come true.

Express It

How effectively are you living in the present moment? Have you been running your life on "if and when" hopes rather than trusting in God's faithfulness? Ask God for both the wisdom and will to see what needs to be done now and for the strength you will need to do it.

Consider It

As you read Genesis 40:1–45:28, consider these questions:

1) About how many years passed between Joseph's dreams and their fulfillment? (See 37:2 and 41:46)

_____

_____

_____

2) What is your impression of Joseph's life in prison?

_____

_____

_____

3) How would you explain the cupbearer's behavior in forgetting Joseph?

_____

_____

_____

4) What are the primary differences between the two trips to Egypt that Jacob's sons made?

_____

_____

_____

5) Why did Joseph treat them the way he did?

_____

_____

_____

6) How did the brothers tell Jacob that his son Joseph, whom he thought was long dead, was really alive?

_____

_____

_____

7) What are the most obvious leadership traits that Joseph displays in these chapters?

_____

_____

_____

Reunited

Family members long separated by tragedies like war or disasters experience almost unspeakable joy in being reunited. Those who believe their loved one is dead find the encounter particularly sweet. Jacob thought Joseph was dead for over 20 years. What a reunion that must have been!

Read Genesis 46:1–49:33

Genesis 46:1–47:31

Joseph Brings His Family to Egypt

46 So Israel took his journey with all that he had and came to Beersheba, and offered sacrifices to the God of his father Isaac. ²And God spoke to Israel in visions of the night and said, "Jacob, Jacob." And he said, "Here am I." ³Then he said, "I am God, the God of your father. Do not be afraid to go down to Egypt, for there I will make you into a great nation. ⁴I myself will go down with you to Egypt, and I will also bring you up again, and Joseph's hand shall close your eyes."

⁵Then Jacob set out from Beersheba. The sons of Israel carried Jacob their father, their little ones, and their wives, in the wagons that Pharaoh had sent to carry him. ⁶They also took their livestock and their goods, which they had gained in the land of Canaan, and came into Egypt, Jacob and all his offspring with him, ⁷his sons, and his sons' sons with him, his daughters, and his sons' daughters. All his offspring he brought with him into Egypt.

⁸Now these are the names of the descendants of Israel, who came into Egypt, Jacob and his sons. Reuben, Jacob's firstborn, ⁹and the sons of Reuben: Hanoch, Pallu, Hezron, and Carmi. ¹⁰The sons of Simeon: Jemuel, Jamin, Ohad, Jachin, Zohar, and Shaul, the son of a Canaanite woman. ¹¹The sons of Levi: Gershon, Kohath, and Merari. ¹²The sons of Judah: Er, Onan, Shelah, Perez, and Zerah (but Er and Onan died in the land of Canaan); and the sons of Perez were Hezron and Hamul. ¹³The sons of Issachar: Tola, Puvah, Yob, and Shimron. ¹⁴The sons of Zebulun: Sered, Elon, and Jahleel. ¹⁵These are the sons of Leah, whom she bore to Jacob in Paddan-aram, together with his daughter Dinah; altogether his sons and his daughters numbered thirty-three.

> # Key Verse
>
> *Israel said to Joseph, "Now let me die, since I have seen your face and know that you are still alive"* (Gen. 46:30).

¹⁶The sons of Gad: Ziphion, Haggi, Shuni, Ezbon, Eri, Arodi, and Areli. ¹⁷The sons of Asher: Imnah, Ishvah, Ishvi, Beriah, with Serah their sister. And the sons of Beriah: Heber and Malchiel. ¹⁸These are the sons of Zilpah, whom Laban gave to Leah his daughter; and these she bore to Jacob—sixteen persons.

¹⁹The sons of Rachel, Jacob's wife: Joseph and Benjamin. ²⁰And to Joseph in the land of Egypt were born Manasseh and Ephraim, whom Asenath, the daughter of Potiphera the priest of On, bore to him. ²¹And the sons of Benjamin: Bela, Becher, Ashbel, Gera, Naaman, Ehi, Rosh, Muppim, Huppim, and Ard. ²²These are the sons of Rachel, who were born to Jacob—fourteen persons in all.

²³The sons of Dan: Hushim. ²⁴The sons of Naphtali: Jahzeel, Guni, Jezer, and Shillem. ²⁵These are the sons of Bilhah, whom Laban gave to Rachel his daughter, and these she bore to Jacob—seven persons in all.

²⁶All the persons belonging to Jacob who came into Egypt, who were his own descendants, not including Jacob's sons' wives, were sixty-six persons in all. ²⁵And the sons of Joseph, who were born to him in Egypt, were two. All the persons of the house of Jacob who came into Egypt were seventy.

Jacob and Joseph Reunited

[28]He had sent Judah ahead of him to Joseph to show the way before him in Goshen, and they came into the land of Goshen. [29]Then Joseph prepared his chariot and went up to meet Israel his father in Goshen. He presented himself to him and fell on his neck and wept on his neck a good while. [30]Israel said to Joseph, "Now let me die, since I have seen your face and know that you are still alive." [31]Joseph said to his brothers and to his father's household, "I will go up and tell Pharaoh and will say to him, 'My brothers and my father's household, who were in the land of Canaan, have come to me. [32]And the men are shepherds, for they have been keepers of livestock, and they have brought their flocks and their herds and all that they have.' [33]When Pharaoh calls you and says, 'What is your occupation?' [34]you shall say, 'Your servants have been keepers of livestock from our youth even until now, both we and our fathers,' in order that you may dwell in the land of Goshen, for every shepherd is an abomination to the Egyptians."

Jacob's Family Settles in Goshen

47 So Joseph went in and told Pharaoh, "My father and my brothers, with their flocks and herds and all that they possess, have come from the land of Canaan. They are now in the land of Goshen." [2]And from among his brothers he took five men and presented them to Pharaoh. [3]Pharaoh said to his brothers, "What is your occupation?" And they said to Pharaoh, "Your servants are shepherds, as our fathers were." [4]They said to Pharaoh, "We have come to sojourn in the land, for there is no pasture for your servants' flocks, for the famine is severe in the land of Canaan. And now, please let your servants dwell in the land of Goshen." [5]Then Pharaoh said to Joseph, "Your father and your brothers have come to you. [6]The land of Egypt is before you. Settle your father and your brothers in the best of the land. Let them settle in the land of Goshen, and if you know any able men among them, put them in charge of my livestock."

[7]Then Joseph brought in Jacob his father and stood him before Pharaoh, and Jacob blessed Pharaoh. [8]And Pharaoh said to Jacob, "How many are the days of the years of your life?" [9]And Jacob said to Pharaoh, "The days of the years of my sojourning are 130 years. Few and evil have been the days of the years of my life, and they have not attained to the days of the years of the life of my fathers in the days of their sojourning." [10]And Jacob blessed Pharaoh and went out from the presence of Pharaoh. [11]Then Joseph settled his father and his brothers and gave them a possession in the land of Egypt, in the best of the land, in the land of Rameses, as Pharaoh had commanded. [12]And Joseph provided his father, his brothers, and all his father's household with food, according to the number of their dependents.

Joseph and the Famine

[13]Now there was no food in all the land, for the famine was very severe, so that the land of Egypt and the land of Canaan languished by reason of the famine. [14]And Joseph gathered up all the money that was found in the land of Egypt and in the land of Canaan, in exchange for the grain that they bought. And Joseph brought the money into Pharaoh's house. [15]And when the money was all spent in the land of Egypt and in the land of Canaan, all the Egyptians came to Joseph and said, "Give us food. Why should we die before your eyes? For our money is gone." [16]And Joseph answered, "Give your livestock, and I will give you food in exchange for your livestock, if your money is gone." [17]So they brought their livestock to Joseph,

and Joseph gave them food in exchange for the horses, the flocks, the herds, and the donkeys. He supplied them with food in exchange for all their livestock that year. [18]And when that year was ended, they came to him the following year and said to him, "We will not hide from my lord that our money is all spent. The herds of livestock are my lord's. There is nothing left in the sight of my lord but our bodies and our land. [19]Why should we die before your eyes, both we and our land? Buy us and our land for food, and we with our land will be servants to Pharaoh. And give us seed that we may live and not die, and that the land may not be desolate."

[20]So Joseph bought all the land of Egypt for Pharaoh, for all the Egyptians sold their fields, because the famine was severe on them. The land became Pharaoh's. [21]As for the people, he made servants of them from one end of Egypt to the other. [22]Only the land of the priests he did not buy, for the priests had a fixed allowance from Pharaoh and lived on the allowance that Pharaoh gave them; therefore they did not sell their land.

[23]Then Joseph said to the people, "Behold, I have this day bought you and your land for Pharaoh. Now here is seed for you, and you shall sow the land. [24]And at the harvests you shall give a fifth to Pharaoh, and four fifths shall be your own, as seed for the field and as food for yourselves and your households, and as food for your little ones." [25]And they said, "You have saved our lives; may it please my lord, we will be servants to Pharaoh." [26]So Joseph made it a statute concerning the land of Egypt, and it stands to this day, that Pharaoh should have the fifth; the land of the priests alone did not become Pharaoh's.

[27]Thus Israel settled in the land of Egypt, in the land of Goshen. And they gained possessions in it, and were fruitful and multiplied greatly. [28]And Jacob lived in the land of Egypt seventeen years. So the days of Jacob, the years of his life, were 147 years.

[29]And when the time drew near that Israel must die, he called his son Joseph and said to him, "If now I have found favor in your sight, put your hand under my thigh and promise to deal kindly and truly with me. Do not bury me in Egypt, [30]but let me lie with my fathers. Carry me out of Egypt and bury me in their burying place." He answered, "I will do as you have said." [31]And he said, "Swear to me"; and he swore to him. Then Israel bowed himself upon the head of his bed.

Go Deeper

Genesis 46:1–5 describes Jacob's departure from the Promised Land to travel for his reunion with Joseph. Two questions arise when we see that he stopped in Beersheba. One is why Beersheba? Secondly, why sacrifice there?

Beersheba was on the direct route to Egypt. It was the jumping-off place before crossing the desert to Egypt. But it also had a role in the family history. It was a worship place. Jacob probably stopped and sacrificed at Beersheba for at least three reasons. First, Beersheba was a favorite encampment; it was a place of the covenant and a place of worship for Jacob's grandfather, Abraham. (See 21:27–34.) Beersheba was a place where

(continued)

Go Deeper Continued . . .

Abraham met with God. It was also a place of covenant and worship for Jacob's father, Isaac. (See 26:23–25.) Both Abraham and Isaac called upon the name of the Lord at Beersheba.

A second reason for stopping at Beersheba involved special memories of God's goodness. Every time one of the patriarchs was in Beersheba, the hand of God was good to him. Before going to Egypt, before he left the Promised Land, Jacob wanted to spend some time in Beersheba because that's where the goodness of God is evident.

The third reason for sacrificing at Beersheba has to do with Jacob seeking guidance and counsel from God. As anxious as he was to see Joseph, Jacob would rather have died in Canaan without seeing Joseph than to leave it without knowing he had God's blessing. He couldn't leave the Promised Land without God's approval, which God gave. (See 46:2–4.)

Are you committed to having God's blessing? So committed that you won't do what you want until you're sure that it's what God will bless? That approach is the foundation for wise living.

M ore than 20 years had passed since Jacob sent Joseph to check on the welfare of his brothers. We have followed Joseph's experiences in Egypt. Our knowledge of Jacob's life during those years is practically blank. We do know the loss of Joseph devastated Jacob. Two decades later, he sent ten of his sons to Egypt for food during a famine but refused to let Benjamin go, "for he feared that harm might happen to him" (42:4). Benjamin was Jacob's only link to Rachel and Joseph.

Finally, toward the end of chapter 46, Jacob and Joseph met again for the first time since Joseph was just 17 years old. It's a very tender passage. "Then Joseph prepared his chariot and went up to meet Israel his father in Goshen. He presented himself to him and fell on his neck and wept on his neck a good while" (46:29). The account of their encounter is reserved, but we can be sure the emotions in that moment were beyond description. For Jacob, the previous two decades must have felt like a huge and painful interruption in his life. Now things were back in order. That's why he could say, "Now let me die, since I have seen your face and know that you are still alive" (v. 30).

Jacob had known for months that Joseph was living. But the news had been almost too good to believe. At first, he hadn't. "And they told him, 'Joseph is still alive, and he is ruler over all the land of Egypt.' And

> *"God loves each of us immeasurably and individually at the same time. God is our surest example of how to love our children. He is the ultimate source of every true blessing and genuine love."*

his heart became numb, for he did not believe them" (45:26). This was an eerie reversal of his experience so long before. Then the sons had brought the infamous coat stained with blood; now they brought wagons and a message from Joseph. Bad news is easier to believe. It takes time for good news to undo the effects of bad news.

Jacob gradually grasped the unbelievable: "But when they told him all the words of Joseph, which he had said to them, and when he saw the wagons that Joseph had sent to carry him, the spirit of their father Jacob revived" (v. 27). But it wasn't until he saw his son and felt his tears running down his neck that Jacob knew that God had set things in order once again. Jacob's response reminds us of Simeon, the aged man in the temple (Luke 2:25–32). When he saw the baby Jesus, he said he could die in peace because he had seen the Lord's salvation. That's how Jacob felt. He'd seen the one who was going to save his family, and he could die in peace.

In Jacob's case, death wouldn't come for another 17 years (Gen. 47:28). Now that the family was reunited, they needed a place to live. Joseph did his best to prepare his family for the cultural differences in Egypt. He carefully instructed them what to say when they were introduced to Pharaoh. They were to explain that they were both cattlemen and sheepherders but to stress the fact that they were cattlemen and not shepherds, because Egyptians considered shepherds the dregs of society. But old habits die hard, and the brothers demonstrated they were not quite ready to take their little brother's instructions to heart (47:3–6). They had a lot to learn from Joseph.

Later, when Jacob realized that he would soon die, he set into motion a custom that had been in the family but which he took to a new level—the giving of the blessing. Genesis 48–49 describes in detail this tradition, which still has great validity today. One of the reasons families should stay united is because this in itself provides a blessing to the next generation. Fathers can have a lasting and powerful impact on their children's lives by giving them blessings—speaking and delivering love and truth into their lives.

How did Jacob bless his sons? He spoke with authority into their lives, demonstrating that he had observed them carefully and considered for a long time what he was going to say. He spoke truth into their lives, describing traits that must have been difficult to face. He spoke hopefully about their future. As he blessed them, he was weaving together not only a family but a nation. Their fate would be experienced together. Genesis 49:28 gives us this summary of Jacob's actions: "All these are the twelve tribes of Israel. This is what their father said to them as he blessed them, blessing each with the blessing suitable to him."

Jacob's life is certainly a warning to parents against playing favorites with children. But how do we give the same love to kids who are so different from each other? Jacob's blessing gives us an important clue: we bless our children by loving each of them in a way that is "suitable" to each one. Wise love notes carefully what a child needs and provides that response. It's how God treats us. He loves each of us immeasurably and individually at the same time. God is our surest example of how to love our children. He is the ultimate source of every true blessing and genuine love.

Express It

One of the issues this lesson brings up is awareness of separations in our lives. Are there people with whom you need to be reunited? What will it take to make that possible? Sometimes, it will take God's direct intervention. As you pray, seek God's guidance about relationships in your life that may need to be reunited.

Consider It

As you read Genesis 46:1–49:33, consider these questions:

1) How did Jacob know it was okay with God to leave the Promised Land and go to Egypt?

2) What have been some of your own cherished experiences of family reunions? Why do these affect us so deeply?

3) What were the eventual results of the famine in Egypt? How was the relationship between Pharaoh and his people altered?

4) Why do you think Jacob chose an unusual order of blessing in handling Joseph's sons?

5) What observations did you make in reading Jacob's blessings over his sons?

6) How did Jacob's arrangements for his burial indicate his priorities?

7) In what ways have you experienced the blessing of your parents? How have you passed it on?

Sovereign Over All

The span of time covered by the Book of Genesis hasn't been equaled since. This book is an indelible lesson in God's ability to demonstrate His sovereignty over the big picture and His participation in the lives of individuals. Genesis sets the stage for everything since.

Read Genesis 50:1–26

50 Then Joseph fell on his father's face and wept over him and kissed him. ²And Joseph commanded his servants the physicians to embalm his father. So the physicians embalmed Israel. ³Forty days were required for it, for that is how many are required for embalming. And the Egyptians wept for him seventy days.

⁴And when the days of weeping for him were past, Joseph spoke to the household of Pharaoh, saying, "If now I have found favor in your eyes, please speak in the ears of Pharaoh, saying, ⁵My father made me swear, saying, 'I am about to die: in my tomb that I hewed out for myself in the land of Canaan, there shall you bury me.' Now therefore, let me please go up and bury my father. Then I will return." ⁶And Pharaoh answered, "Go up, and bury your father, as he made you swear." ⁷So Joseph went up to bury his father. With him went up all the servants of Pharaoh, the elders of his household, and all the elders of the land of Egypt, ⁸as well as all the household of Joseph, his brothers, and his father's household. Only their children, their flocks, and their herds were left in the land of Goshen. ⁹And there went up with him both chariots and horsemen. It was a very great company. ¹⁰When they came to the threshing floor of Atad, which is beyond the Jordan, they lamented there with a very great and grievous lamentation, and he made a mourning for his father seven days. ¹¹When the inhabitants of the land, the Canaanites, saw the mourning on the threshing floor of Atad, they said, "This is a grievous mourning by the Egyptians." Therefore the place was named Abel-mizraim; it is beyond the Jordan. ¹²Thus his sons did for him as he had commanded them, ¹³for his sons carried him to the land of Canaan and buried him in the cave of the field at Machpelah, to the east of Mamre, which Abraham bought with the field

Key Verse

And Joseph said to his brothers, "I am about to die, but God will visit you and bring you up out of this land to the land that he swore to Abraham, to Isaac, and to Jacob" (Gen. 50:24).

from Ephron the Hittite to possess as a burying place. ¹⁴After he had buried his father, Joseph returned to Egypt with his brothers and all who had gone up with him to bury his father.

God's Good Purposes

¹⁵When Joseph's brothers saw that their father was dead, they said, "It may be that Joseph will hate us and pay us back for all the evil that we did to him." ¹⁶So they sent a message to Joseph, saying, "Your father gave this command before he died, ¹⁷'Say to Joseph, Please forgive the transgression of your brothers and their sin, because they did evil to you.' And now, please forgive the transgression of the servants of the God of your father." Joseph wept when they spoke to him. ¹⁸His brothers also came and fell down before him and said, "Behold, we are your servants." ¹⁹But Joseph said to them, "Do not fear, for am I in the place of God? ²⁰As for you, you meant evil against me, but God meant it for good, to bring it about that many people should be kept alive, as they are today. ²¹So do not fear; I will provide for you and your little ones." Thus he comforted them and spoke kindly to them.

The Death of Joseph

[22]So Joseph remained in Egypt, he and his father's house. Joseph lived 110 years. [23]And Joseph saw Ephraim's children of the third generation. The children also of Machir the son of Manasseh were counted as Joseph's own. [24]And Joseph said to his brothers, "I am about to die, but God will visit you and bring you up out of this land to the land that he swore to Abraham, to Isaac, and to Jacob." [25]Then Joseph made the sons of Israel swear, saying, "God will surely visit you, and you shall carry up my bones from here." [26]So Joseph died, being 110 years old. They embalmed him, and he was put in a coffin in Egypt.

Go Deeper

Joseph was deeply affected by his brothers. They continued to expect revenge from him. They had never completely forgiven themselves, so their guilt haunted them. Joseph gave them strong assurances of his forgiveness, and he displayed a very beautiful trait: his willingness to release a debt owed to him without requiring that the debt be paid. He said, "Do not fear, for am I in the place of God? As for you, you meant evil against me, but God meant it for good, to bring it about that many people should be kept alive, as they are today" (50:19–20).

If there were nothing else in this whole story of Joseph that would make him seem an Old Testament foreshadow of Christ, this statement would do it.

Joseph is a finger pointing toward the Lord Jesus. Joseph shows us what forgiveness is all about. Forgiveness isn't making people grovel before us. Forgiveness isn't beating out of them a confession of their sin. Forgiveness is releasing them from the debt of their guilt and going about our business.

Jesus did that for you and me. If He did it for us, shouldn't we be able to do it for one another? Certainly! Ever since Eden, humans have persisted in finding ways to do evil. Yet God has persisted in turning evil intentions into something very good. Let Him do that for you too.

Genesis begins in Eden and ends in Egypt. It begins with hope (3:15) and ends with hope (50:24). Genesis starts with God creating the earth from nothing, and it concludes with God turning evil into good. Now, that's the grace of God—to make something out of nothing and then to make good out of evil. All beginnings trace their roots back to Genesis. Each of us is a living result of events in Genesis. And in the beginning of Genesis, we find God.

In the Book of Genesis we find a great purpose, a great promise and a chosen people. All three belong to God. As Creator, He has a purpose for the creation and each part of it. As God, He can make an unbreakable promise because He alone has everything it might take to bring it to pass. As Sovereign, He can choose a person through whom to birth a people whom He chooses for special duties. In Genesis we not only have the creation, but also God setting into motion the plan that will lead to re-creation, when the Son of God will make all things new.

What an amazing story—that a God who can create the universe with a word in an instant chose to work out His plan through plodding and sinful men generation after generation. What an exciting story— one in which God repeatedly snatched His plan out of the jaws of failure at the last moment.

The vast wideness of creation funnels down until we meet a solitary man named Abraham. God sees potential in him. God decides to make something great out of him. So, God sends him on a journey of faith.

Although faith is preferable by far to unbelief and willful ignorance, faith isn't easy. Abraham had to wait. God's promise hinged on a child, and every passing year accumulated in Sarah and Abraham's life made the promise seem more implausible. They even tried some shortcuts to assist God, but God's plan still ran its course.

Isaac was the miracle child born to two ancient characters. The mocking laughter gave way to joyful laughter when *Laughter* (Isaac) was born. Isaac and his wife, Rebekah, gave birth to wrestling twins, and they struggled most of their lives. But God had chosen Jacob to carry the promise forward.

Jacob gave birth to 12 sons who became the nation of Israel. Two of Jacob's sons were singled out for special duties, one immediate and the

> *"Whatever else we may face in the future, difficult or delightful, we can be sure that God will visit us. He will draw our attention, lead us and eventually bring us to the place He has planned for us."*

other long-term. Judah, though born fourth in line, became the father of the tribe from which the royal line was taken. Judah was father to kings and to the King of kings, Jesus. Joseph was chosen to ensure the survival of the family, bearing the hardship of betrayal, slavery, injustice and unfairness to rise to the second-highest seat in Egypt. He secured the well-being of his family, though his brothers had tried to kill him.

The final chapter of Genesis ushered in a 430-year period of silence. In that chapter, the unbreakable link between the people of Israel and the Promised Land was forged in a unique way. The last patriarch, Jacob, died in Egypt but was buried back in Canaan. Joseph eventually died in Egypt but insisted that his embalmed body and coffin be held until the people left Egypt. Joseph was so sure that God's plan would succeed that he reserved a place among the departing people to have his remains returned to the Promised Land. Joseph's faith shines down through history. "Then Joseph made the sons of Israel swear, saying, 'God will surely visit you, and you shall carry up my bones from here'" (50:25). In the heat of Egyptian slavery God forged a people He persisted in calling His own.

Twice in this chapter Joseph has looked into the future and used the phrase "God will visit you" (vv. 24–25). His words ring true for every life, in every generation, including yours and mine. Whatever else we may face in the future, difficult or delightful, we can be sure that God will visit us. He will draw our attention, lead us and eventually bring us to the place He has planned for us. Immediate circumstances are rarely a reliable indication of God's presence.

We've seen over and over in Genesis that God works even in the worst situations to bring about His will. Our faith must be anchored in the immovable rock of God's sovereignty. The greatest example of the truth of Joseph's statement happened one night in Bethlehem of Judea, when God visited the earth bodily and took up temporary residence here to work out the heart of the promise He made in Genesis, that through Abram's seed all the world would be blessed. The God who visits, teaches, dies on a cross and rises again is the God Joseph was describing. He is the God we trust.

Express It

Genesis reveals the lives of real people, as real as we are today. These are not nice, antiseptic, pseudo-righteous people. Their holiness is full of grit. Their experience with God is truthful even when it's ugly. Pray that you won't waste your time trying to pacify God or treat Him as if He didn't know everything about you. God wants to meet us in the depth of where and who we really are.

Consider It

As you read Genesis 50:1–26, consider these questions:

1) How did Joseph handle his father's death?

_____

_____

_____

2) What did the brothers think after they returned from burying Jacob?

_____

_____

_____

3) What did Joseph say and do in response to their fears?

_____

_____

_____

4) How would you illustrate the truth Joseph stated—that God can take what others mean for evil and turn it into good?

_____

_____

_____

5) In what way does Genesis 50:20 foreshadow Jesus' life and death?

_____

_____

_____

6) What do you think of the way Joseph emphasized his confidence in God described in the last three verses of Genesis?

_____

_____

_____

7) Which persons and what insights from Genesis have had the deepest impact on your life during this study?

_____

_____

_____